WALLABY

The Cheers™ Bartending Guide

by Marcia Rosen and Gerry Hunt

Charles/Burrows/Charles Production
in Association with Paramount Television

A WALLABY BOOK
Published by Simon & Schuster, Inc.
NEW YORK

ACKNOWLEDGMENTS

The authors would like to extend a special thanks to Louis R. Mastrianna, Denise Tratolatis, Pat Clarke, John Crosbie, and Herb Rosen whose assistance was invaluable in writing this book.

CONTENTS

Introduction

Hi. Sam Malone here, owner, proprietor, and main magnificent pagan beast of television's favorite bar—Cheers. But more about me later. First I'd like to tell you about my favorite bar, which has its own fascinating history.

The "Cheers" bar you see on television really does exist. It's in the center of Boston, on the corner of Beacon and Brimmer between Charles and Arlington streets, and it's called the Bull and Finch. The Bull and Finch was voted "Best Neighborhood Bar in Boston" by *Boston* magazine, won the coveted title of having the "Best Bloody Mary in Boston" for six successive years, and is now expected to be retired to the barroom hall of fame. The "Cheers" set is an authentic reproduction of the Bull and Finch in just about every detail, right down to the cigar-store Indian, the moose head on the wall, the old lamps, stained-glass windows, and even the triangle hanging over the bar.

But how did the Bull and Finch become Cheers? Well, our producer was vacationing in Boston when he decided to take in a few neighborhood bars to get some color and ideas for the "Cheers" set. While he was strolling down Boston's famous Beacon Street, he stopped in the small cellar bar under the old Hampshire Hotel and he immediately fell in love with it. The rest is television history.

Our model for Cheers was originally built in 1911 as a private townhouse known as the Thayer Mansion (even though our television Cheers sign shows the date as 1895). It became the Hampshire House in 1942 and the Bull and Finch in 1969. The bar is an exact replica of an old English pub. Owner Tom Kershaw scouted British public houses (that's why they're called "pubs") until he found exactly what he was looking for. The oak bar, its ornate fittings and brass rails, and even the pub's interior, including beams and pews, were re-created in England by British craftsmen. Then the whole ball game was shipped back to Boston to become the Bull and Finch.

Hundreds of photographs were taken of the Bull and Finch, and it was rebuilt inch by inch by the set designers and craftsmen at Paramount studios in Hollywood. The Bull and Finch that you see in a still shot at the beginning of the show is the real thing.

Cheers is almost an exact reproduction of the Bull and Finch, with only one difference—the bar at the Bull and Finch is against a wall, while the Cheers bar has an island you can walk around. It gives more freedom of movement and a better background for the on-camera action.

Which, I might add, there is plenty of. I mean, of which there is plenty. Thank you, Diane. Diane is the newest addition to the Cheers staff and holds a brand new position—Learned Wait-ress. Certainly not without her considerable feminine charms, Diane, former teaching assistant and current effete snob, has the sometimes annoying tendency to overintellectualize the slicing of a lemon. (She also knows nothing about baseball!) But, as hard as she tries to hide it, I can tell that beneath that icy exterior, there lurks the passion of a wolverine in heat. (It takes a man like me to bring out the best in a woman.) She's a terrific kid, though, and gets along with everyone. . . .

Except maybe, Carla. Ah, Carla. Diane and Carla, Carla and Diane . . . Well, I guess it's safe to say that two drowning cats in a bag are more friendly to each other than these two. Carla's not what you'd call the bookish type, nor subtly beautiful in that classic way. Carla's what you'd call . . . earthy. Though husbandless, Carla leads a rich family life—five children and one on the way (constantly it seems). She's a good waitress and a good friend.

And there's Coach. Coach is my best friend—everyone's best friend—and was my pitching coach when I was still playing ball. Now he's my bartender and there's not another one like him—and that's not just because he's been hit in the head once too often. It's true that Coach gets a little confused sometimes, but everyone says he makes them feel right at home (figure that one out!), and his heart sure is in the right place.

Norm and Cliff are two of our most regular customers. Cliff's the neighborhood mail carrier, and darn proud of it, too. He also knows more trivial facts and long-forgotten anecdotes than the *Book of Lists* or Ripley's Believe It or Not. Norm's an accountant, but even he loses track of the number of beers he drinks here at Cheers.

That's one thing about Norm. He does love his beer. In fact, he'll be giving all of you aspiring bartenders the scoop on beers and ales. Cliff gives you lots of toasts, so you'll have plenty of excuses to hoist a few, while Carla helps with those hangover blues. Diane has deigned to impart to you her dieting tips for the drinker, and Coach shows you the tools of the bartending trade.

Oh, I almost forgot. I'm Sam Malone, formerly Sam "Mayday" Malone, relief pitcher for the Boston Red Sox. That was before I damaged my elbow—by bending it too often at the bar. In other words, I was an alcoholic. But I gave up drinking, and baseball, and now I'm here, making delicious drinks and seducing gorgeous members of the opposite sex. (What a life!) I'll be showing you my tried-and-true drink recipes, both alcoholic and nonalcoholic, that will make your parties great successes. As for seducing gorgeous members of the opposite sex, I'm afraid you're on your own.

Well, welcome to Cheers, and have fun. The first drink is on Coach. . . .

1

COACH'S TIPS ON TOOLS OF THE TRADE

You know, I once coached a kid who could do it all. Hit the ball out of the park, run a mile and shag a fly, slide like greased lightning. But he didn't make the big leagues. Why? He was always in such a rush, he'd run on the field without his pants.

What? That sounds silly? Well, a ballplayer without his pants is like a bartender without ice cubes. I mean, to do the job right, your bar's gotta be suited up for any occasion. And having the right equipment is the biggest part of running a first-rate bartending team. Just buying the booze isn't enough.

You gotta have the right glasses, gadgets, garnishes, flavorings, mixers, and mineral waters. And you gotta know where everything is beforehand.

Now, I know that's a ton of stuff to remember all at once. But if I can do it—uh . . . what was I saying?

Oh yeah, I always check out my work area to see if everything is in order. That way, if it's all there, I know I have it.

Let's see. It looks pretty good. No . . . wait a minute. I can't find my aspirins. You see, I always get these headaches. Must have been that last pitch!

Now, if you've got a minute, I'd like to tell you everything I know about working behind the bar. I've even written some of it down.

Actually, I didn't do it all, Sam helped. But, I hope you follow the suggestions. I know I should.

GLASSES

You can't pour a drink without having a glass to put it in. Try it sometime if you don't believe me. And not only do you need a glass, but it has to be the *right* glass.

If it's too small and filled to the brim, it could get real messy the first time somebody takes a sip.

If it's too big, the small amount of liquor inside makes you look like a cheapskate.

And if you keep serving full 5-ounce drinks in tall glasses, you'll have a roomful of drunks in no time.

Here's a list of all-purpose glasses that will get you through any occasion.

Beer	(12 ounces)	Mug	(10–12 ounces)
Brandy snifter	(6–12 ounces)	Old-fashioned	(6–10 ounces)
Champagne	(5–6 ounces)	Pony	(1 ounce)
Claret	(4 ounces)	Sauterne	(4 ounces)
Cocktail	(2–3½ ounces)	Sherry	(2–2½ ounces)
Cordial	(¾–1 ounce)	Shot	(1–1½ ounces)
Goblet	(8–12 ounces)	Tom Collins	(10–14 ounces)
Highball	(8–10 ounces)	Whiskey	(1–2½ ounces)

The truth is a bartender just can't have enough glasses. You never know when some clumsy oaf, like myself, will drop a tray and break a bunch, or if the entire Fenway Park crowd will all decide to drop in for a drink. Anyway, the more the better. But if you're just beginning to stock your bar, the best and most inexpensive way to begin is with the basics. At least a dozen of each of the four types listed below should get you rolling:

Old-fashioned glasses. These are used for drinks poured on the rocks or served neat (without ice).

Highball glasses. These get a lot of use behind the bar for a variety of drinks. If you're making something mild, or whipping up a specialty that calls for lots of ice, plenty of soda or other mixer, these glasses are perfect.

Wineglasses. These can range from small to very large. The small sizes (4 to 6 ounces) are good for serving aperitifs and cocktails (if you don't already have special glasses for them), and the large sizes (8 to 16 ounces) are good to use with most wines.

Goblets. These are probably the most practical because they'll stand up to any mixed drink as well as beer and wine.

Then, after you've had a little practice behind the bar, you can add the fancier styles. That's how I did it. Now, I have to try to convince the guys to drink something besides beer.

GADGETS

These are the basic gadgets that no good bartender would be without. I use them every day, or try to. Matter of fact, I don't know how I ever kept my ties clean before Sam got me the blender.

Although it seems like a lot, most of the things, like spoons and measuring cups, are inexpensive—and you'll probably find that you already have them. The special items, like the blender, food processor, juicer, and ice crusher, can always be added later. And when you do, here's a piece of advice: never let a machine know when you're in a hurry.

Bar muddler (for crushing sugar cubes and mint)
Bottle and beer can opener
Cocktail napkins and coasters
Cocktail shaker and wire strainer
Corkscrew
Double-ended measure (to pour 1-ounce pony
    and 1½-ounce jigger shots)
Electric blender
Food processor
Ice bucket and tongs
Ice crusher
Lemon stripper
Lime squeezer
Long spoon or glass stirring rod
Measuring spoons
Paring knife and cutting board
Pitcher
Straws
Toothpicks

GARNISHES AND FLAVORINGS

Some garnishes, like lemons, limes, and orange peels, are used to make a drink look classy. Others, like the onion in the

Gibson, the lemon twist in the Rob Roy, and the olive in the martini, make these drinks what they are. Flavorings, like grenadine and bitters, can really liven up the taste of a carefully mixed drink.

So, the next time you're planning a party, don't forget these important touches. I've never seen a well-stocked bar without them.

Bitters. These are tangy mixers used to "kill" the sweetness of a drink. Angostura bitters are probably the best known.

Citrus fruit (lemons, limes, and oranges). Citrus slices should be cut thin, less than 1/4 inch thick. Orange slices should be halved. Use a lemon stripper if you only need the peel. Use fresh fruit when you can get it. Otherwise canned, bottled, and frozen is all right.

Cocktail onions. For use in Gibsons. Drain before adding.

Maraschino cherries. Lots of people like them, even though they don't add anything to a drink.

Nonalcoholic fruit-flavored sweeteners. Those such as grenadine and orgeat are popular for punches and drinks.

Olives, celery, cinnamon sticks, and nutmeg. These odds and ends always come in handy for use in several drinks.

Sugar. When mixing a drink, use only the finest granulated sugar called "superfine," unless the recipe calls for something different.

MINERAL WATERS AND MIXERS

The other day a customer told me I was slipping because his favorite brand of bourbon and water tasted like an old sweat sock. After making sure I had my shoes on, I checked the drink.

Well, the bourbon was fine, but the water . . . phew! It could have knocked out Ali at thirty paces.

If you live in an area where there are problems with the water, it's a good idea to keep the bottled brand around for use in your bar.

Light liquors, like vodka, gin, and rum, usually go well with a variety of mixers, and I'll list a few of these below.

Club soda. You'll be surprised to know this mixer is more popular than water. Because it has a mild flavor, it goes well with almost any drink.

Colas. These soft drinks mix well with many liquors, particularly rum, besides being well liked on their own.

Ginger ale. This tangy-flavored beverage can really perk up the spirits, making it many people's favorite mixer.

Grapefruit juice. You couldn't make a Salty Dog without it.

Lemon juice. An indispensable mixer for many drinks.

Lime juice. This can be mixed with a variety of liqueurs.

Orange juice. Orange juice goes with practically everything.

Quinine (tonic) water. This bittersweet beverage mixes well with everything, from gin, to vodka, rum, and whiskey.

Tomato juice. If your friends like Bloody Marys, you should keep several quarts on hand. Once opened, jars are best for storage in the refrigerator.

If you still have any doubt about what to use, just remember the stronger the flavor of the mixer, as in colas and juices, the more it will mask the taste of the liquor.

DRINK TIPS AND TECHNIQUES

You know what I always tell people who ask my advice on mixing drinks? Do nothing. I mean, don't do anything unless the recipe tells you.

Lots of first-time bartenders feel like experimenting. But the only way to turn out a fireball of a drink is to follow the directions. Every now and then I remember the first few drinks I made as a new bartender and the memory still brings tears to my eyes—but not because they were that good. So, only use the ingredients and the measurements that are listed in the recipes. Believe me . . . I learned the hard way. And so did my customers.

Sam wrote me up a chart which he says is guaranteed to take the guesswork out of my job. Now I can't make a mistake even if I wanted to.

Here are the rules:

1. Always mix the ingredients in the right order. Never overestimate and never overpour. When a drink calls for sugar, put the sugar in the glass first because it won't dissolve quickly enough in the liquor alone. Then add a few drops of water or mixer, and stir until the sugar is melted. Fruit juices should come next, because they also have to be blended into the drink, followed by the alcohol and then the ice. The mixer should be the last thing added. The only time you'd want to put in the ice before the alcohol is after you've been bartending a while and can measure with your eye instead of with your tools. This can get tricky, because the ice in the glass creates an optical illusion making you either overpour or underpour. Are you following me?

2. Follow the recipe:

To stir. Clear spirits, like gin and vodka, bubbly beverages, like champagne, and drinks of different densities, should be stirred with ice for best results.

To shake. If the recipe calls for ingredients that don't mix easily, like eggs, cream, or fruit juices, they should be shaken or put into an electric blender to give the drink a smooth, creamy texture.

To strain. This is always a good idea for cocktails because it keeps those loose bits of ice from falling into the glass.

To pour. This may sound like a piece of cake, but there is a trick to getting equal consistency when mixing a batch of drinks. Put the glasses in a row and fill each only halfway. Then start from the beginning again, and fill each glass to the top. This will spread the ingredients evenly, so each glass gets an equal amount.

To float liqueurs. Liqueurs vary in density and thickness, and certain ones will float on top of others. There are two ways to float liqueurs. The easiest way is to pour several liqueurs into one glass and refrigerate. After an hour, each liqueur will find its own weight level. Another way is to pour each liqueur slowly over the back part of a bar spoon into a glass. The spoon gives the liquids a chance to settle on top of one another.

To flame liqueurs. This can get tricky. So you must be very careful. The key is to have all your utensils and ingredients prewarmed before igniting.

3. Always prechill glasses, liquor, and mixers because most drinks taste best when served icy cold. The easiest way to do this is to refrigerate the utensils and ingredients at least one hour before serving. But, if you don't have enough time, here's a quick cooling tip: simply wet the glasses and place them in the freezer for five minutes while you continue making the drink. Then remove the glasses, wipe them on the outside with a dry towel, and pour.

4. Don't guess—always check your measurements.

If the recipe calls for	*It means*
1 cup	8 ounces
1 dash	3 drops
1 dollop	a good-sized splash
1 fifth	25.6 ounces
3 fingers	3 ounces
1 jigger	1½ ounces
1 pint	16 ounces
1 pony	1 ounce
1 shot	1–1½ ounces
Splash	a generous spoonful
1 split	6–8 ounces
1 tablespoon	½ ounce
1 teaspoon	⅙ ounce
Touch	a few drops
Wineglassful	4 ounces or ½ cup

These measurements might come in handy for punches and eggnogs:

Average bottle of wine	26 ounces
Demijohn	1–10 gallon jug
Jeroboam (4 bottles)	104 ounces
Magnum (2 bottles)	52 ounces
Methuselah (8 bottles)	208 ounces
Quart of champagne	27 ounces
Rehoboam (6 bottles)	156 ounces
Split of champagne	6½ ounces

Some other helpful equivalents:

1 average lemon	=	3 tablespoonsful juice
1 average lime	=	2 tablespoonsful juice
1 tablespoon reconstituted lemon juice	=	juice of ½ average lemon
1 teaspoon egg white	=	3–4 drops egg white substitute
1 ice tray	=	1 quart crushed ice
1 whole medium orange	=	⅓ cup juice

5. Don't forget your garnishes and flavorings. (See the section on garnishes and flavorings, page 16.)

STOCKING YOUR LIQUOR CABINET

Here's a handy list of basic beverages to stock any average-sized bar. Sam and I have tried to cover every category, and with these you should be able to make almost any drink in the book. (Remember, they are only suggestions. Let your own taste and pocketbook be your final coach.)

APERITIFS AND VERMOUTHS
Aperitifs (3 bottles of your own choice)
French dry vermouth (3 bottles)
Italian sweet vermouth (3 bottles)

BEER AND WINE
Beer (2) 6-pack
Stout (1) 4-pack
Ale (1) 6-pack
Dry red wine (3 bottles)
Dry white wine (6 bottles)

FLAVORLESS SPIRITS
Gin (1 bottle)
Tequila (1 bottle)
Vodka (1 bottle)

REGIONAL SPIRITS
Blended whiskey for mixed drinks (3 bottles)
Bourbon or rye whiskey (1 bottle)
Brandy (3 bottles of your choice for mixed drinks)
Cognac (1 bottle for sipping)
Liqueurs (3 bottles of your choice)
Medium-dry sherry or dry sherry (1 bottle)
Port (1 vintage bottle)
Rum (1 bottle)
Scotch (2 bottles—one light, one heavy)

HOW MANY BOTTLES TO BUY

You say you're ready to give a party, but you don't know how much alcohol to buy? No problem. I took this chart right out of Sam's little black book (after I copied a few phone numbers!). He says it (the chart, that is) has never failed. And you won't either.

Just remember the most important thing. After you've got everything ready and waiting, don't forget to unlock the door and let the people in.

NUMBER OF PEOPLE

	4	6	8	10	20	30	40	
Aperitifs*	1	2	2	3	5	8	10	N
Brandies/Liqueurs* (for afterdinner sipping in 1-ounce servings)	1/2	1/2	1	1	2	2	4	U M B E R
Champagne*	2	2	3	4	7	10	13	O F
Spirits (2-ounce servings)	1	2	2	3	5	8	10	B O T
Wine (if served during dinner)	3	4	6	7	13	19	25	T L E S

Note: These bottle estimates are based on each guest having 2 to 3 glasses. For nonalcoholic mixers, plan on a pint bottle per person. And with beer, figure 2 to 3 bottles or cans per person.
*The estimates for these drinks are based on fifth-sized bottles.

2

SAM'S DRINK RECIPES

It's no secret that I'm kind of an expert when it comes to baseball, beautiful women, and bartending. Well, maybe there are one or two other guys in the world who know as much as I do, but they're not as cute.

But seriously, no matter what game I'm playing, I try to be the best. My sinkers are legendary, my record with the ladies, matchless. And now I'm going to tell you my secret to great bartending. It's all the same strategy—terrific timing. Get that down right and you're home free.

Like when you sneak in your slider . . . get the outside corner . . . and set that baby down right where you want it. You've gotta be just as careful with the way you pick and choose your brews. Especially if you're planning on a big party or trying to impress someone special.

Sometimes it could be as easy as opening a can. And knowing when to bring out the cocktails, the afterdinner brandies, and the liqueurs doesn't require a college degree. But, what about a brunch, when you want some early-morning eye-openers? Aperitifs and wines are low in alcohol and, for that reason, are good bets for a mellow morning. The same goes for any light, wine-based mix, as long as it's not too sweet.

Drinks in tall glasses are first-class thirst quenchers and go great in the afternoon, or late evening. Fizzes, Collinses, and highballs are all easy to make. And certain cocktails, such as martinis, Manhattans, and daiquiris, are perfect for both picnics and parties because they can be premixed in large batches, saving you a lot of time and trouble later on at the bar. Face it, who wants to be fussing around with stirrers and straws while there's other, more "social" life going on.

And for those cold winter afternoons, nothing will stoke your stomach better than a hot, relaxing drink and brandy, rum, and whiskey are the most popular of these. Warm them up, and snuggle down with a special friend.

Now that you know when to serve 'em, fixing the drink is the easiest part. There are over 300 terrific recipes that can be easily prepared for any occasion. They're all here, so all you have to do is call in some friends and say, "Cheers."

APERITIFS

I know what you're thinking. You'd never drink anything you couldn't pronounce first. Well, maybe an aperitif isn't as American sounding as a martini (though when you really get down to it, just how American does "martini" sound?!). But more people who want to keep in shape are switching to these mild drinks instead of having their usual five-to-seven-o'clock bracers.

The classic lightweights are vermouth (sweet and dry) and sherry. But, if these sound too much like something you'd serve your great-aunt from Cleveland, there are the popular French favorites: Dubonnet (red and white), Lillet (red and white), St. Raphael (red and white), and Byrrh (pronounced *beer*), which certainly sound chic enough, even for Diane.

If you feel like going Italian, there's Campari, Punt e Mes, and Cynar (pronounced *she-nar*). And if you're in the mood for something that'll knock your socks off, try Pernod and Ricard from France, and ouzo from Greece. Stronger than brandy, these drinks should be served with water or club soda on the side, to smooth out the taste, and dilute the liquor a bit. The following recipes make one drink, unless the recipe says otherwise.

ADONIS

2 ounces dry sherry
1 ounce sweet vermouth
1 dash orange bitters

Fill a mixing glass with ice. Add all ingredients and stir vigorously. Strain into a cocktail glass.

AMERICANO COCKTAIL

3 ounces sweet vermouth
1½ ounces Campari
1 twist of lemon or orange peel

Fill a mixing glass with ice. Combine vermouth and Campari and stir to mix well. Strain into a cocktail glass and garnish with twist of lemon or orange peel.

BOB DANBY

2 ounces Dubonnet
1 ounce brandy

Fill a mixing glass with ice. Add ingredients and stir until mixed. Strain into cocktail glass.

BRAZIL

1 1/2 *ounces sherry*
1 1/2 *ounces dry vermouth*
1 *dash Pernod*
1 *dash angostura bitters*
1 *twist of lemon peel*

Fill a mixing glass with ice. Add all ingredients except lemon peel and stir vigorously. Strain into a cocktail glass and garnish with twist of lemon.

BUTTONHOOK

1/2 *ounce Pernod*
1/2 *ounce apricot brandy*
1/2 *ounce brandy*
1/2 *ounce white crème de menthe*

Fill a cocktail shaker with ice. Add all ingredients and shake vigorously. Strain into a cocktail glass.

BYRRH CASSIS

1 1/2 *ounces Byrrh*
1/4 *ounce crème de cassis*
1/2 *ounce fresh lemon juice*
1 *lemon slice*

Fill a cocktail shaker with ice. Add all ingredients except lemon slice and shake vigorously until well blended. Strain mixture into an ice-filled old-fashioned glass. Garnish with lemon.

BYRRH COCKTAIL

1 1/2 *ounces Byrrh*
1 1/2 *ounces gin*
1 *twist of lemon peel*

Fill a cocktail shaker with ice. Add Byrrh and gin and stir until well mixed. Strain into an ice-filled glass and garnish with twist of lemon.

CAMPARI AND SODA

1¹/₂ ounces Campari
Club soda
1 twist of lemon peel

Fill a tall glass with ice cubes. Pour Campari over the ice and add club soda to taste. Garnish with twist of lemon.

CHAMPAGNE FRAISE

¹/₂ teaspoon kirsch
¹/₂ teaspoon strawberry liqueur
4 ounces chilled Brut champagne
1 strawberry with stem

Chill tulip-shaped wineglass. Mix kirsch and strawberry liqueur until well blended. Tilt wineglass and pour liqueur mixture down the side. Swirl to coat entire glass. Add chilled champagne and garnish with fresh strawberry.

CINZANO

3 ounces Cinzano sweet vermouth
2 dashes orange bitters
1 orange peel

Fill a cocktail shaker with ice. Add Cinzano and orange bitters and mix well. Strain into a cocktail glass. Twist orange peel over the drink and drop into the glass.

DIABLO

1¹/₂ ounces port
1¹/₂ ounces dry vermouth
2 dashes lemon juice

Fill a mixing glass with ice. Pour port and dry vermouth over the ice. Add lemon juice and mix well. Strain into a cocktail glass.

DIPLOMAT

3 ounces dry vermouth
1 ounce sweet vermouth
1 dash Maraschino
1 lemon peel
1 Maraschino cherry

Fill a mixing glass with ice. Pour dry and sweet vermouth and the Maraschino over the ice and stir vigorously to mix well. Strain into a cocktail glass, twist the lemon peel over drink, and drop it in the glass. Garnish with cherry.

DUBONNET MANHATTAN

1½ ounces Dubonnet
1½ ounces blended whiskey
1 lemon slice
1 Maraschino cherry

Fill a mixing glass with ice. Add Dubonnet and whiskey and stir vigorously until blended. Strain into a chilled glass. Garnish with lemon slice and cherry.

DUBONNET ON THE ROCKS

1 twist of lemon peel
4 ounces Dubonnet

Put a twist of lemon peel in the bottom of a chilled old-fashioned glass. Add 3 or 4 ice cubes. Pour Dubonnet directly over the ice.

EAST INDIA COCKTAIL

1½ ounces sweet sherry
1½ ounces dry vermouth
1 dash orange bitters

Fill a cocktail shaker with ice. Pour sherry and vermouth over the ice. Add orange bitters. Shake until well blended and pour into a chilled sherry glass.

FIG LEAF

1¹/2 ounces sweet vermouth
1 ounce white rum
1 tablespoon lime juice
1 dash angostura bitters

Fill a cocktail shaker with ice. Pour vermouth, rum, and bitters over the ice. Stir vigorously. Add lime juice and shake vigorously until well mixed. Strain into a frosted cocktail glass.

ITALIAN COCKTAIL

3 ounces Punt e Mes
1 dash dry vermouth
1 dash Campari
1 lemon wedge
1 lemon slice

Put 3 ice cubes in a large wineglass. Add dry vermouth and Campari to the Punt e Mes, stirring until mixed well. Pour the combined ingredients over the ice. Squeeze the lemon wedge over the glass, then drop into drink. Garnish with slice of lemon.

KIR

4 ounces chilled dry white wine
¹/2 ounce crème de cassis

Put 2 ice cubes in a chilled wineglass. Pour ingredients over the ice and stir a couple of times.

MACARONI

1¹/2 ounces Pernod
¹/2 sweet vermouth

Fill a cocktail shaker with ice. Pour ingredients over the ice and shake vigorously until well mixed. Strain into a chilled cocktail glass.

MIMOSA

3 ounces freshly squeezed orange juice
3 ounces chilled Brut champagne

Combine ingredients in a chilled tulip-shaped wineglass.

NEGRONI

1 1/2 ounces sweet vermouth
1 1/2 ounces Campari
1 1/2 ounces gin
1 lemon peel

Fill a mixing glass with ice. Add sweet vermouth, Campari, and gin and stir vigorously until well mixed. Strain into an ice-filled old-fashioned glass. Twist lemon peel over the drink and drop it in the glass.

NINE-PICK

1 ounce Pernod
1 ounce curaçao
1 ounce brandy
1 egg yolk, room temperature

Fill a cocktail shaker with ice and add all the ingredients. Shake vigorously until well blended. Strain into a chilled cocktail glass.

NINETEEN-PICK-ME-UP

1 1/2 ounces Pernod
3/4 ounce gin
1 dash angostura bitters
1 dash orange bitters
1 dash sugar syrup (such as Karo)
1 dash club soda

Fill a cocktail shaker with ice. Add all the ingredients except club soda and shake until well blended. Strain into a chilled cocktail glass. Add club soda.

PANSY

1 1/2 ounces Pernod
6 dashes grenadine
2 dashes angostura bitters

Fill a cocktail shaker with ice. Add Pernod and grenadine and shake until well blended. Strain into a chilled cocktail glass. Add angostura bitters.

PERNOD I

2 ounces Pernod
1/2 ounce water
1 dash angostura bitters
1 dash heavy sugar syrup

Fill a cocktail shaker with ice. Add all ingredients and shake until well mixed. Pour into a chilled cocktail glass.

PERPETUALLY YOURS

1 1/2 ounces sweet vermouth
1 1/2 ounces dry vermouth
2 dashes crème de cacao
4 ounces crème de cassis

Fill a mixing glass with ice. Add the ingredients, one at a time, and stir until well blended. Strain into a chilled cocktail glass.

PINEAPPLE COCKTAIL

1 cup crushed pineapple
6 ounces dry white wine
3 ounces fresh pineapple juice
1 tablespoon lemon juice
9 ounces sherry
6 small pineapple wedges

Soak a cup of crushed pineapple in white wine for 2 hours. Pour wine, juices, and sherry into an ice-filled cocktail shaker. Chill the mixture well. Shake vigorously and chill for another 1/2 hour. Strain the mixture into 6 chilled cocktail glasses and garnish with pineapple wedges. Serves 6.

PLAIN SHERRY COCKTAIL

3 ounces sherry
2 dashes Maraschino
2 dashes Pernod

Fill a cocktail shaker with ice. Add all the ingredients and shake until well blended. Strain into a chilled cocktail glass.

PLAIN VERMOUTH

15 ounces dry vermouth
1 teaspoon Pernod
1 teaspoon Maraschino
6 Maraschino cherries

Fill a mixing glass with ice. Add all ingredients except Maraschino cherries. Stir until well mixed and strain into 6 cocktail glasses. Garnish with cherries. Serves 6.

QUEEN ELIZABETH WINI

1 ounce dry vermouth
1¹/₂ ounces Benedictine
1 tablespoon lime or lemon juice

Fill a mixing glass with ice. Add all ingredients and stir vigorously until well blended. Strain into a chilled cocktail glass.

ST. RAPHAEL AND VODKA

1¹/₂ ounces vodka
3 ounces St. Raphael
Sparkling mineral water
1 lemon peel

Put 3 or 4 ice cubes in a large wineglass. Pour vodka and St. Raphael over the ice. Add a splash of sparkling mineral water and stir gently. Twist lemon peel over the drink and drop into glass.

SLOE VERMOUTH

1 ounce sloe gin
1 ounce dry vermouth
1 ounce fresh lemon juice
1/2 lemon slice

Fill a cocktail shaker with ice. Add all ingredients except lemon slice and shake until well mixed. Strain into a cocktail glass and garnish with lemon slice.

**SOUL KISS
COCKTAIL**

1 1/2 ounces Dubonnet
1 1/2 teaspoons fresh orange juice
3/4 ounce dry vermouth
3/4 ounce bourbon
1/2 orange slice

Fill a cocktail shaker with ice. Add all ingredients except orange slice to the shaker and shake vigorously until well blended. Strain into a chilled cocktail glass. Garnish with orange slice.

VERMOUTH CASSIS

3 ounces dry vermouth
1 ounce crème de cassis
Splash of sparkling water
1 lemon slice

Fill a tall glass with ice cubes. Add vermouth and crème de cassis and stir until blended. Add a splash of sparkling water, stir gently, and garnish with slice of lemon.

**VERMOUTH
COCKTAIL**

1 ounce sweet vermouth
1 ounce dry vermouth
1 dash of orange bitters
1 Maraschino cherry

Fill a mixing glass with ice cubes. Add all ingredients except cherry and stir well. Strain into cocktail glass and garnish with Maraschino cherry.

VERMOUTH ON THE ROCKS

4 ounces sweet or dry vermouth

Fill an old-fashioned glass with ice. Add the preferred vermouth.

VICTORY

1½ ounces Pernod
1½ ounces grenadine
Splash of club soda

Fill a cocktail shaker with ice. Add Pernod and grenadine and shake until well blended. Strain into a chilled cocktail glass and add splash of club soda. Stir gently.

WEEP NO MORE

1½ ounces Dubonnet
1¼ ounces brandy
1½ ounces lime juice
1 dash Maraschino

Fill a mixing glass with ice. Add all ingredients and stir until well blended. Strain into a cocktail glass.

WHISPERS OF THE FROST

¾ ounce port
¾ ounce sherry
¾ ounce blended whiskey
1 lemon slice
1 orange slice

Fill a mixing glass with ice. Add port, sherry, and whiskey and stir until well blended. Strain into a cocktail glass. Garnish with lemon and orange slices.

YORK SPECIAL *3 ounces dry vermouth*
1 ounce Maraschino
4 dashes orange bitters
1 Maraschino cherry

Fill a mixing glass with ice. Add vermouth, Maraschino, and bitters and stir until well blended. Strain into a cocktail glass. Garnish with cherry.

BRANDY

Depending on whether you're after a good sipping brandy, or simply want a cocktail mixer, there is a big diffrence in the types of liquors you should be looking for. The better the brandy, the more it's going to cost. So before you waste a week's salary on a savory aroma just to spike the party punch, here are a few things you probably want to know about brandy.

Aging is the key, usually from three to nine years, that separates the good from the bad. And the way you can tell that is by looking at the label. If you want the kind of brandy that you can enjoy slowly after a meal, look for a V.S.O.P. designation. You will find this mostly on imported brands, such as Martell, Courvoisier, and Rémy Martin, to name a few. None of these should ever be diluted.

V.S. (aged five to seven years) means Very Superior.

V.S.O.P. (aged over seven years) means Very Superior Old Pale, or, in other words, top quality.

And, if these don't please your palate, you can try the cadillacs of the line, Napoleon (Courvoisier) or Cordon Bleu (Martell).

While you're at it, don't get confused by the stars on the labels, thinking that they represent the quality inside the bottle. What they do indicate for the majority of brands is grade. However, there are some exceptions, like Metaxa (from Greece) and Carmel (from Israel).

For example, a seven-star Metaxa does mean top-of-the-line quality, equal to a Napoleon. A five-star Metaxa rates a V.S.O.P. as does the five-star Carmel. And an unstarred Metaxa matches a V.S. rating. But beyond those two—buyer, beware.

If you're planning a party and need some good mixing brandies, try some of the domestics. They're perfect on the rocks, with soda, for cooking and flaming. But while these are good, they lack the woody bite that makes the imported brands able to stand up on their own.

Now that about covers the wine-based brandies. The fruit-based brandies fall into a different category, since they're mostly used as cordials. When selecting one, let your own taste be your guide.

The following recipes serve one unless otherwise indicated.

AMERICAN BEAUTY

3/4 ounce brandy
3/4 ounce dry vermouth
3/4 ounce orange juice
1 dash white crème de menthe
1 dash grenadine
1 ounce port

Fill a cocktail shaker with ice. Pour all ingredients except port over the ice and shake vigorously until well blended. Strain into a chilled cocktail glass. Pour port slowly down the side of the glass so that it floats on top.

BOMBAY

1 ounce brandy
1/2 ounce sweet vermouth
1/2 ounce dry vermouth
1 teaspoon curaçao
1 dash Pernod

Fill a shaker with ice. Pour all ingredients over the ice and shake vigorously until well blended. Strain into a cocktail glass.

BRANDY AND SODA

2 ounces brandy
Club soda to taste

Fill a chilled highball glass with ice. Pour brandy over ice and add club soda. Stir gently.

BRANDY COLLINS

2 ounces brandy
2 teaspoons superfine sugar
1 ounce fresh lemon juice
Club soda
1 lemon slice
1 orange slice
1 Maraschino cherry

Fill a cocktail shaker with ice and add first 3 ingredients. Place 2 ice cubes in a tall glass and pour the mixed ingredients into it. Fill the glass with club soda and garnish with fruit.

BRANDY FIZZ

3 ounces brandy
1 tablespoon superfine sugar
2 tablespoons lemon juice
1 tablespoon lime juice
Club soda to taste
1 lime slice

Fill a cocktail shaker with ice. Add first 4 ingredients and shake vigorously until blended. Strain into a tall glass containing 2 ice cubes. Add club soda to taste. Garnish with lime.

BRANDY FLIP

1 egg
1 teaspoon superfine sugar
2 teaspoons heavy cream
3 ounces brandy
Freshly grated nutmeg

Fill a cocktail shaker with ice. Beat egg, sugar, and cream together until pale yellow. Pour brandy into the mixture and stir slightly. Pour over ice in the shaker and shake vigorously until frothy. Garnish with nutmeg.

BRANDY HIGHBALL

2 ounces brandy
Ginger ale or mineral water
1 lemon peel

Fill a highball glass with ice. Add brandy and fill the glass with ginger ale or mineral water. Twist a peel of lemon over the drink and drop it in glass.

BRANDY MANHATTAN

2 ounces brandy
1/2 ounce sweet vermouth
1 dash angostura bitters
1 Maraschino cherry

Fill a cocktail mixer with ice. Add all ingredients except cherry and stir until well mixed. Strain into a chilled cocktail glass. Garnish with Maraschino cherry.

BRANDY OLD-FASHIONED

1 sugar cube
2 dashes of angostura bitters
1 teaspoon water
3 ounces brandy
1 lemon peel

Stir sugar, bitters, and water in an old-fashioned glass until sugar is dissolved. Add ice to fill. Pour brandy over ice and stir until well mixed. Twist lemon peel over the drink and drop it in glass.

BRANDY SLING I

1 teaspoon superfine sugar
2 tablespoons fresh lemon juice
2 ounces brandy

Place sugar and lemon juice in bottom of a cocktail mixer. Stir until sugar is dissolved. Add ice cubes to fill and pour brandy over the ice. Stir until well blended. Strain into a chilled cocktail glass.

BRANDY SLING II

1 teaspoon superfine sugar
1/2 ounce lemon juice
1/2 ounce orange juice
2 ounces brandy
1/2 orange slice

Place sugar, lemon juice, and orange juice in a cocktail mixer. Stir until sugar is dissolved. Add ice cubes to fill and pour brandy over the ice. Stir until well blended. Strain into a chilled cocktail glass and garnish with orange slice.

CARROL COCKTAIL

1 1/2 ounces brandy
1/4 ounce sweet vermouth
1 Maraschino cherry

Fill a cocktail mixer with ice. Add brandy and vermouth and stir until well blended. Garnish with cherry.

CHERRY BLOSSOM

2 teaspoons fresh lemon juice
1/4 teaspoon orange curaçao
1/4 teaspoon grenadine
1 1/4 ounces brandy
3/4 ounce cherry brandy
1 Maraschino cherry

Place first 3 ingredients in bottom of a cocktail shaker. Stir until well blended. Add ice cubes to fill and pour brandies over ice. Shake until well blended. Strain into cocktail glass. Garnish with Maraschino cherry.

CLASSIC

1 tablespoon lemon juice
1 teaspoon superfine sugar
1 ounce brandy
1/2 ounce orange curaçao
1/2 ounce Maraschino
1 lemon peel

Fill a mixing glass with ice. Add lemon juice and sugar and stir until sugar dissolves. Add remaining ingredients except peel and stir vigorously. Strain into chilled glass that has been dipped in lemon juice and sugar. Twist peel over drink and drop into glass.

DEAUVILLE

1/2 ounce brandy
1/2 ounce calvados

1/2 ounce Cointreau
1 teaspoon lemon juice

Fill a cocktail mixer with ice. Pour all ingredients into mixer and stir vigorously until well blended. Strain into a cocktail glass.

FANTASIO

1 ounce brandy
3/4 ounce dry vermouth
1 teaspoon white crème de menthe
1 teaspoon Maraschino

Fill a cocktail mixer with ice. Pour all ingredients into mixer and stir vigorously until well blended. Strain into a cocktail glass.

HARVARD

1 1/2 ounces brandy
3/4 ounce sweet vermouth
2 tablespoons lemon juice
1 dash angostura bitters
1 teaspoon grenadine

Fill a cocktail mixer with ice. Pour all ingredients into mixer and stir vigorously until well blended. Strain into a cocktail glass.

JACK ROSE

2 ounces calvados
1/2 ounce fresh lime juice

Fill a cocktail shaker with ice. Add ingredients and shake vigorously until well blended. Strain into cocktail glass.

LADY BE GOOD

1 ounce brandy
1/2 ounce sweet vermouth
1/2 ounce white crème de menthe

Put 1/2 cup cracked ice in a shaker, add all ingredients and shake vigorously. Strain into a chilled glass.

MIKADO

1 ounce brandy
1 dash Triple Sec
1 dash grenadine
1 dash crème de noyau
1 dash angostura bitters

Fill an old-fashioned glass with ice. Pour all ingredients over ice and stir until well blended.

NONE BUT THE BRAVE

1¹/2 ounces brandy
1 ounce Jamaica ginger beer
1 dash lemon juice
1 teaspoon superfine sugar

Fill a cocktail shaker with ice. Add all ingredients and shake vigorously until well blended. Strain into a cocktail glass.

PHOEBE SNOW

2 ounces brandy
³/4 teaspoon Pernod
2 ounces Dubonnet

Fill a cocktail mixer with ice cubes. Pour all ingredients over ice. Strain into a chilled cocktail glass.

POOP DECK

1 ounce brandy
¹/2 ounce blackberry brandy
¹/2 ounce port

Fill a cocktail shaker with ice. Add all ingredients and shake vigorously until well blended. Strain into a cocktail glass.

SIDECAR

2 ounces brandy
¹/2 ounce Cointreau

1/2 ounce lemon juice
1/2 lemon slice

Fill a cocktail shaker with ice. Add all ingredients and shake vigorously until well blended. Strain into a chilled cocktail glass. Garnish with lemon slice.

SIR WALTER

1 1/2 ounces brandy
3/4 ounce white rum
1 teaspoon orange curaçao
1 teaspoon grenadine
1 teaspoon lemon juice
1/2 lemon slice
1/2 lime slice

Fill a cocktail shaker glass with cracked ice. Combine all ingredients and shake vigorously until well blended. Strain into a chilled cocktail glass. Garnish with lemon and lime slices.

SOMERSET

1 1/2 ounces brandy
1/2 ounce cherry brandy
2 dashes angostura bitters
2 dashes heavy sugar syrup

Fill a cocktail mixing glass with ice. Combine all ingredients and stir vigorously until well blended. Strain into a chilled cocktail glass.

STINGER

1 1/2 ounces brandy
1/2 ounce white crème de menthe

Fill a cocktail shaker with cracked ice. Combine all ingredients and shake vigorously until well blended. Strain into a chilled cocktail glass.

THUNDER	1 egg yolk
	1 teaspoon heavy cream
	1 pinch cayenne pepper
	3 ounces brandy

Beat egg yolk, heavy cream, and cayenne pepper until egg mixture is light yellow. Fill a cocktail shaker with ice. Pour in brandy and add egg mixture. Shake vigorously until well blended. Strain into a chilled cocktail glass.

WILLIAM OF	1 1/2 ounces brandy
ORANGE	3/4 ounce orange curaçao
	3/4 ounce orange bitters

Fill a cocktail mixing glass with ice. Combine all ingredients and stir vigorously until well blended. Strain into a chilled cocktail glass.

GIN

There are probably more famous drinks made out of gin than any other liquor. Cliff tells me that the Dutch originated this happy combination of distilled grain flavored with juniper berries. But we Americans did the next best thing—invented the martini.

As the story goes, a bartender in San Francisco, during the days of the Gold Rush, cooked it up as a morning-after cure for a hungover customer. The potion of gin and vermouth worked so well, the grateful Mr. Martinez spread the word of the miracle cocktail far and wide.

The proportions then took some strange turns throughout the years, but I think it tastes better without the Maraschino and the jigger of beer. Today's trend for ardent martini drinkers is to make it drier and drier, meaning anywhere from five parts gin to one part vermouth, to sixteen parts gin to one part vermouth.

When talking about a martini, the word *dry* means less vermouth. When talking about "dry" on the gin label, and practically all U.S. gins use this word, it means lacking in sweetness. (And when you're talking about humor, dry means Diane.)

Probably the only other thing you need to know about gin is that it can be made in two ways: by compounding, which is mixing the neutral spirit with juniper berries; or by distilling, which is simply processing the neutral spirit. (And Americans must really have the spirit, because all our gins are distilled.)

Again, all recipes make one serving.

ALEXANDER II

1 ounce gin
1/2 ounce white crème de cacao
1/2 ounce heavy cream

Fill a cocktail shaker with ice and add all ingredients. Shake vigorously until well blended and frothy. Strain into a cocktail glass.

ALLEN

1 1/2 ounces gin
3/4 ounce Maraschino
1 dash lemon juice

Fill a cocktail mixing glass with ice and add all ingredients. Stir until well blended. Strain into a chilled cocktail glass.

BACHELOR BAIT

2 ounces gin
$^1/_2$ teaspoon grenadine
1 egg white
1 dash orange bitters

Fill a cocktail shaker with ice and add all ingredients. Shake vigorously until well blended and frothy. Strain into a cocktail glass.

BEE'S KNEES

$1^1/_2$ ounces gin
1 teaspoon honey
1 tablespoon lemon juice

Fill a cocktail mixing glass with ice and add all ingredients. Stir until well blended. Strain into a chilled cocktail glass.

BENNETT COCKTAIL

1 teaspoon superfine sugar
$^1/_2$ ounce fresh lime juice
2 ounces gin
2 dashes angostura bitters
1 lime peel

Stir sugar into lime juice until dissolved. Fill cocktail shaker with ice. Add sweetened lime juice and other ingredients. Shake vigorously until well blended. Strain into a chilled cocktail glass. Twist lime peel over drink and dropto in the glass.

BISHOP'S COCKTAIL

2 ounces gin
2 ounces ginger wine

Fill a cocktail mixing glass with ice and add ingredients. Stir until well blended. Strain into a chilled cocktail glass.

BLOODHOUND

1/2 ounce dry vermouth
1/2 ounce sweet vermouth
1 ounce gin
2 strawberries with stems

Fill a cocktail shaker with ice. Add all ingredients except strawberries. Shake vigorously until well blended. Strain into a chilled cocktail glass. Garnish with strawberries.

BRONX

1 1/2 ounces gin
1/2 ounce fresh orange juice
1/4 ounce dry vermouth
1/4 ounce sweet vermouth
1 orange slice

Fill a cocktail shaker with ice. Add all ingredients except orange slice. Shake vigorously until well blended. Strain into a chilled cocktail glass. Garnish with orange slice.

GIN BULLSHOT

2 ounces gin
3 ounces chilled beef bouillon

Fill a cocktail shaker with ice. Add all ingredients and shake until well blended and chilled. Strain into an ice-filled old-fashioned glass.

BUNNY HUG

1 ounce gin
1 ounce whiskey
1 ounce Pernod

Fill a cocktail shaker with ice. Add all ingredients and shake until well blended and chilled. Strain into a chilled cocktail glass.

CABARET COCKTAIL

1 1/2 ounces gin
1/2 teaspoon dry vermouth
1/4 teaspoon Benedictine
2 dashes angostora bitters
1 Maraschino cherry

Fill a cocktail mixing glass with ice. Combine all ingredients, except Maraschino cherry. Stir until well blended. Strain into a chilled cocktail glass. Garnish with cherry.

CHELSEA SIDECAR

2 ounces gin
1 ounce Triple Sec
1 1/2 tablespoons lemon juice

Put 1/2 cup cracked ice in a cocktail shaker. Add all ingredients and shake vigorously until well blended. Strain into a chilled cocktail glass.

CLUB

2 ounces gin
3/4 ounce sweet vermouth
1 green olive

Fill a cocktail mixer with ice. Add gin and vermouth and stir until well blended. Strain into a cocktail glass. Garnish with green olive.

DAMN THE WEATHER

1 1/2 ounces gin
3/4 ounce sweet vermouth
3/4 ounce orange juice
1 1/2 teaspoons curaçao

Put cracked ice in a cocktail shaker. Add all ingredients and shake vigorously until well blended. Strain into a chilled cocktail glass.

DELMONICO

1¹/2 ounces gin
1 ounce dry vermouth
1 dash orange bitters
1 orange peel

Fill a cocktail mixer with ice. Add gin, vermouth, and orange bitters. Swirl gently to blend. Strain into a cocktail glass. Twist the orange peel over the drink and drop into glass to garnish.

DUBONNET COCKTAIL

1¹/2 ounces gin
1¹/2 ounces Dubonnet Red
1 dash orange bitters
1 lemon peel

Fill a cocktail mixer with ice. Add gin, Dubonnet, and bitters and stir until well blended. Strain into a cocktail glass. Twist lemon peel over the drink and drop into glass.

GIBSON

1 dash dry vermouth
2¹/2 ounces gin
1 cocktail onion

Fill a cocktail mixer with ice. Pour vermouth over the ice and add gin. Stir gently until well blended and chilled. Strain into a chilled cocktail glass and garnish with cocktail onion.

GIMLET

2¹/2 ounces gin
2 ounces Rose's lime juice

Fill a cocktail mixer with ice. Add gin and lime juice and stir until ingredients are well blended. Strain into a chilled cocktail glass.

GIN AND CIN

2¹/2 ounces gin
1¹/2 ounces red Cinzano

Pour ingredients into a cocktail glass and stir. This drink is served at room temperature.

GIN AND TONIC

1¹/2 ounces gin
Quinine water to taste
1 lime wedge

Fill a highball glass with ice. Pour gin over ice and add quinine water to taste. Stir gently to mix. Squeeze lime juice into drink. Lime may be left in drink.

GIN FIZZ

1 tablespoon superfine sugar
1 ounce lime juice
1 ounce fresh lemon juice
2 ounces gin
Club soda to taste

Stir sugar, lime, ounce fresh lemon juice and lemon juice together until sugar is dissolved. Fill a cocktail shaker with ice and add gin and sweetened juices and shake vigorously. Strain into an ice-filled highball glass and add club soda.

GIN HIGHBALL

2 ounces gin
Ginger ale or sparkling mineral
water to taste
1 lemon peel

Fill a highball glass with ice. Pour gin over ice and stir to chill. Add ginger ale or sparkling mineral water to taste. Twist lemon peel over the drink and drop it into glass.

GIN RICKEY

Juice of 1/2 lime
2 ounces gin
Sparkling mineral water to taste

Fill a highball glass with ice. Squeeze lime over the ice and drop into the glass. Add gin and sparkling mineral water to taste. Stir gently to blend the ingredients well.

GIN SLING

1 teaspoon superfine sugar
2 tablespoons lemon juice
2 ounces gin
Sparkling mineral water to taste

Stir sugar into lemon juice until sugar is dissolved. Fill a highball glass with ice. Pour lemon juice mixture over it. Add gin and stir to chill ingredients. Add sparkling mineral water to taste and stir gently to blend.

GIN SOUR

1 tablespoon superfine sugar
2 tablespoons lemon juice
2 ounces gin
1 orange slice
1 lemon slice
1 Maraschino cherry

Stir sugar into lemon juice until sugar is dissolved. Fill a cocktail shaker with ice and pour lemon juice mixture and gin over the ice. Shake vigorously. Strain into a chilled sour glass and garnish with slices of fruit and Maraschino cherry.

GRAND PASSION

2 ounces gin
1 ounce passion fruit syrup
1 dash angostura bitters

Fill a cocktail mixing glass with ice. Add all ingredients and stir until ingredients are well blended. Strain into a cocktail glass.

GREAT SECRET

1½ ounces gin
½ ounce red Lillet
1 dash angostura bitters
1 twist of orange peel

Combine all ingredients except orange peel in a mixing glass and stir well. Strain into a cocktail glass and garnish with peel.

LADYFINGER

1 ounce gin
½ ounce kirsch
½ ounce brandy

Fill a cocktail mixing glass with ice. Add all ingredients and stir until ingredients are well blended. Strain into a cocktail glass.

LEAP YEAR

1½ ounces gin
¼ ounce sweet vermouth
¼ ounce Grand Marnier
1 dash lemon juice
1 twist of lemon peel

Fill a cocktail mixing glass with ice. Add all ingredients except lemon peel and stir until ingredients are well blended. Strain into a cocktail glass and garnish with twist.

LOVE

2 ounces sloe gin
½ teaspoon lemon juice
1 egg white
½ teaspoon raspberry brandy
1 twist of lemon peel

Fill a cocktail shaker with ice. Add all ingredients except lemon peel and stir until ingredients are well blended. Strain into a cocktail glass and garnish with twist.

MAGNOLIA

3 ounces gin
1/2 teaspoon grenadine
2 tablespoons lemon juice
1 ounce heavy cream

Fill a cocktail shaker with ice. Pour gin over the ice. Mix grenadine and lemon juice together and stir in heavy cream. Add to gin in shaker and shake vigorously until frothy and well blended. Strain into chilled cocktail glass.

MAIDEN'S BLUSH

2 ounces gin
1 teaspoon orange curaçao
1/4 teaspoon lemon juice
1 teaspoon grenadine

Fill a cocktail shaker with ice. Pour gin and all other ingredients over the ice. Stir a couple of times to blend and then shake vigorously to mix ingredients well. Strain into a cocktail glass.

MARTINI

1/2 ounce dry vermouth
2 ounces gin
1 green olive

Fill a cocktail mixing glass with ice. Pour in dry vermouth and then add gin. Stir gently until mixture is well chilled. Strain into a chilled cocktail glass and garnish with green olive.

MARTINI (DRY)

1/3 ounce dry vermouth
2 ounces gin
1 green olive

Fill a cocktail mixing glass with ice. Pour in dry vermouth and then add gin. Stir gently until mixture is well chilled. Strain into a chilled cocktail glass and garnish with green olive.

MARTINI (EXTRA DRY)

1 splash dry vermouth
2 ounces gin
1 green olive

Fill a cocktail mixing glass with ice. Pour in dry vermouth and then add gin. Stir gently until mixture is well chilled. Strain into a chilled cocktail glass and garnish with green olive.

MR. MANHATTAN

4 mint leaves
1 sugar cube
3 ounces gin
1 teaspoon lemon juice
1 teaspoon orange juice

Place mint leaves in bottom of the cocktail shaker and muddle them with a slightly moistened (add a drop of water) sugar cube. Add remaining ingredients, stirring gently to mix. Shake vigorously until well blended and strain into a cocktail glass. A fresh sprig of mint may be used as a garnish.

MULE'S HIND LEG

1/2 ounce gin
1/2 ounce applejack
1/2 ounce maple syrup
1/2 ounce Benedictine
1/2 ounce apricot brandy

Fill a mixing glass with ice. Pour all ingredients over the ice and stir until well blended. Strain into a cocktail glass.

ORANGE BLOSSOM

1 1/2 ounces gin
2 tablespoons orange juice
1 pinch superfine sugar
1 orange wedge
1 orange slice

Fill a cocktail shaker with ice. Add all ingredients except orange wedge and orange slice. Shake vigorously until well blended. Rub the edge of a cocktail glass with orange wedge and dip in sugar. Strain the drink into the glass and garnish with orange slice.

PINK GIN
2 ounces gin
2 dashes angostura bitters

Fill a mixing glass with ice. Pour ingredients over the ice and stir until well blended. Strain into a cocktail glass.

PINK LADY
1 1/2 ounces gin
1/4 ounce lime juice
1 egg white, chilled
1 teaspoon heavy cream
1 teaspoon grenadine

Fill a cocktail shaker with ice. Add all ingredients and shake vigorously until frothy and well blended. Strain mixture into a chilled cocktail glass.

ROYAL GIN FIZZ
2 ounces gin
2 tablespoons lemon juice
1 teaspoon superfine sugar
1 egg
Club soda to taste

Fill a cocktail shaker with ice. Add all ingredients except club soda. Shake vigorously. Strain mixture into an ice-filled high-ball glass and fill with club soda.

SENSATION
1 1/2 ounces gin
1 tablespoon lemon juice
1 teaspoon Maraschino
1 sprig fresh mint

Fill a cocktail shaker with ice. Add all ingredients except mint and shake vigorously until well blended. Strain mixture into a cocktail glass and garnish with fresh mint.

SINGAPORE SLING

1 teaspoon superfine sugar
2¹/₂ ounces lime juice
1¹/₂ ounces gin
1 ounce cherry brandy
Club soda
1 lime slice

Fill a cocktail shaker with ice. Add sugar to lime juice and stir. Add gin and brandy and shake vigorously until well blended. Strain mixture into a tall glass half filled with ice, add club soda to fill, and garnish with lime slice.

SLOE GIN FIZZ

¹/₂ teaspoon superfine sugar
³/₄ ounce lemon juice
2–3 ounces sloe gin
Club soda
1 lemon slice

Fill a cocktail shaker with ice. Add sugar to lemon juice and stir. Add gin and shake vigorously until well blended. Strain mixture into a tall glass half filled with ice, add club soda to fill, and garnish with lemon slice.

TOM COLLINS

2 teaspoons superfine sugar
3 ounces fresh lemon juice
1¹/₂ ounces gin
Club soda
1 lemon slice
1 orange slice
1 Maraschino cherry

Fill a cocktail shaker with ice. Add sugar to lemon juice and stir. Add gin and shake until well blended. Strain mixture into a tall glass half filled with ice, add club soda to fill, and garnish with fruit.

RUM

According to Cliff, rum got its name from the word *rumbullion,* meaning "rumpus." And history proves that this dynamite party drink has lived up to its name—it certainly has in this bar!

In fact, Cliff tells me that while some people are still under the impression that tea fired our spirit for independence in '76, it was rum that got the war off to such a rousing start. It seems the patriots were gathered around a bowl of rum punch one night, protesting the British tax. The drunker they got, the angrier they got. And in what seemed like no time at all, the solution hit them in a splash of good cheer. The rest is history.

Rum is distilled from sugarcane. And it can be broken down into two categories:

Heavy bodied. Having a strong bouquet and strong molasses taste. Favorite dark rums come from Jamaica, Trinidad, Martinique, and Demerara.

Light bodied. Having a light molasses taste which comes in two varieties—white and gold. The favored light rums come from Puerto Rico and the Virgin Islands.

The following recipes make one serving each.

BACARDI SPECIAL

1 1/2 ounces light rum
3/4 ounces gin
1 1/2 tablespoons lime juice
1 teaspoon grenadine

Swirl all ingredients with ice in a mixing glass until well blended. Strain into a cocktail glass.

BANANA DAIQUIRI

2 ounces light rum
1/2 ounce crème de bananes
1/2 ounce lime juice
1/2 small banana, sliced

Fill an electric blender with 1/2 cup crushed ice. Add all ingredients and blend at high speed until smooth. Serve in a champagne glass or wine goblet.

BEACHCOMBER

2 ounces light rum
1/2 ounce dry vermouth
1/2 ounce sweet vermouth
2 dashes Maraschino

Fill a mixing glass with ice. Add all ingredients and stir. Strain into a chilled cocktail glass.

BLACK DEVIL

2 1/2 ounces light rum
1/2 ounce dry vermouth
1 black olive

Fill a mixing glass with ice. Add rum and vermouth and stir. Strain into a cocktail glass and garnish with black olive.

CASABLANCA

2 ounces golden rum
1 dash angostura bitters
1 teaspoon lime juice
1/4 teaspoon orange curaçao
1/4 teaspoon Maraschino

Fill a cocktail shaker with ice and add all ingredients. Shake vigorously until well blended. Strain into a cocktail glass.

FROZEN DAIQUIRI

2 ounces light rum
2 1/2 ounces lime juice
1/2 tablespoon superfine sugar

Fill an electric blender with all ingredients. Add 1/2 cup crushed ice and blend at high speed until smooth. Pour into a champagne glass or wine goblet.

FROZEN PASSION FRUIT DAIQUIRI

1 1/2 ounces light rum
1/2 ounce passion fruit syrup
1/2 ounce lime juice
1/2 ounce orange juice
1/4 ounce lemon juice

Fill an electric blender with all ingredients. Add 1/3 cup crushed ice and blend at low speed until smooth. Pour into a champagne glass.

FROZEN PINEAPPLE DAIQUIRI

1 1/2 ounces light rum
1/2 ounce lime juice
1/2 teaspoon sugar
4 pineapple chunks

Fill an electric blender with all ingredients. Add 1/3 cup crushed ice and blend at low speed until smooth. Pour into a saucer champagne glass.

FROZEN STRAWBERRY DAIQUIRI

1 1/2 ounces light rum
1/2 ounce strawberry liqueur
1/2 cup sliced strawberries
1/2 ounce lemon juice
1 teaspoon superfine sugar
1 fresh strawberry with stem

Fill an electric blender with all ingredients except fresh strawberry. Add 1/3 cup crushed ice and blend at low speed until smooth. Pour into a saucer champagne glass or wine goblet. Garnish with fresh strawberry.

HAVANA CLUB

1 1/2 ounces light rum
3/4 ounce dry vermouth

Fill a mixing glass with ingredients and stir well. Strain the mixture into a chilled cocktail glass.

HOT BUTTERED RUM I

2 ounces dark rum
1/2 teaspoon superfine sugar
1 lemon peel
1 cinnamon stick
2 whole cloves
1 teaspoon sweet butter
6 ounces cider
Nutmeg

Fill an 8-ounce mug with ingredients except butter, nutmeg, and cider. Then add butter and cider and stir well. Dust with nutmeg.

HOT RUM AND CHOCOLATE

6 ounces hot chocolate
1 1/2 ounces light rum
Whipped cream
Orange rind, grated
Cocoa

Fill an 8-ounce mug two-thirds full with hot chocolate. Add rum and stir gently. Top with whipped cream. Sprinkle on orange rind and dust with cocoa.

HURRICANE

1 ounce dark rum
1 ounce light rum
2 teaspoons lime juice
1 tablespoon passion fruit syrup

Fill a cocktail shaker with ice. Add all ingredients and shake thoroughly. Strain into a cocktail glass.

MAITAI

2 ounces dark rum
2¹/₂ ounces lime juice
¹/₄ teaspoon Triple Sec
1 tablespoon superfine sugar
1 pineapple spear

Fill a cocktail shaker with ice. Add all ingredients except pineapple and shake well. Strain into a tall glass filled with cracked ice. Garnish with pineapple stick.

MONKEY'S PAW

1¹/₂ ounces dark rum
3 ounces pineapple juice
Sparkling mineral water

Fill a tall glass with ice. Add all ingredients and stir gently.

PIÑA COLADA

1¹/₂ ounces light rum
1 ounce cream of coconut
3 ounces pineapple juice
1 pineapple spear

Fill an electric blender with rum, cream of coconut, and juice. Add ¹/₂ cup crushed ice and blend at low speed until smooth. Pour into a tall glass. Garnish with fruit.

PLANTER'S PUNCH

1 tablespoon lime juice
2 tablespoons lemon juice
3 ounces orange juice
1 ounce light rum
1¹/₂ ounces dark rum
¹/₂ ounce grenadine
2 dashes Triple Sec
1 lemon slice
1 orange slice
1 pineapple spear
1 mint sprig

Fill a tall glass with crushed ice. Add fruit juices, grenadine, and light rum and stir until glass is frosted. Add dark rum, stir again, and top with grenadine and Triple Sec. Garnish with the fruit and mint.

QUARTERDECK

1¹/₂ ounces dark rum
³/₄ ounce sherry
1 teaspoon lime juice

Fill a mixing glass with ice. Add all ingredients and stir gently. Strain into a cocktail glass.

RUM DUBONNET

³/₄ ounce light rum
³/₄ ounce Dubonnet Blonde
1¹/₂ tablespoons lime juice

Fill a mixing glass with ice. Add all ingredients and stir well. Strain into a cocktail glass.

RUM DUBONNET DARK

1¹/₂ ounces dark rum
³/₄ ounce Dubonnet
1 teaspoon lime juice
1 lime peel

Fill a cocktail shaker with ice. Add all ingredients except lime peel and shake well. Strain into a chilled cocktail glass and shake well. Twist lime peel over drink and drop into glass.

RUM GIMLET

2¹/₂ ounces light rum
¹/₂ ounce lime juice

Fill a mixing glass with ice. Add ingredients and stir well. Strain into a chilled cocktail glass.

RUM HIGHBALL

1¹/₂ ounces light rum
Sparkling mineral water
1 lemon peel

Fill a highball glass with ice and add rum. Fill to top with mineral water and stir gently. Twist lemon peel over drink and drop into glass.

RUM MARTINI

¹/₂ ounce dry vermouth
2¹/₂ ounces light rum
1 lemon peel

Fill a mixing glass with ice. Add vermouth. Then gently stir in rum until well chilled. Strain into a cocktail glass, twist peel over drink, rub the rim of the glass with peel, and drop into drink.

RUM ON THE ROCKS

2 ounces light rum
1 twist of lemon peel

Fill an old-fashioned glass with ice. Pour on rum and drop in lemon peel.

RUM SOUR

1½ ounces light rum
2½ ounces lemon juice
1 tablespoon superfine sugar
1 orange slice
1 Maraschino cherry

Fill a cocktail shaker with ice. Add rum, lemon juice, and sugar. Shake thoroughly and pour into a sour glass. Garnish with orange slice and cherry.

SCORPION

2½ ounces light rum
2 ounces orange juice
1½ ounces lemon juice
1 ounce brandy
½ ounce orgeat
1 orange slice

Fill an electric blender with all ingredients except orange slice. Add ⅓ cup crushed ice and blend at low speed until smooth. Pour into a highball glass filled with ice cubes. Garnish with orange.

SHANGHAI

1½ ounces dark rum
½ ounce anisette
¾ ounce lemon juice
2 dashes grenadine

Fill a mixing glass with ice. Add all ingredients and stir well. Strain into a cocktail glass.

XYZ

1 ounce dark rum
¾ ounce Cointreau
¾ ounce lemon juice

Fill a cocktail shaker with ice. Add all ingredients and shake well. Strain into a cocktail glass.

ZOMBIE
3/4 ounce 90-proof rum
1 1/2 ounces golden rum
3/4 ounce light rum
3/4 ounce pineapple juice
3/4 ounce papaya juice
3 tablespoons lime juice
1 teaspoon superfine sugar
1 pineapple spear
1 Maraschino cherry
1 tablespoon Demerara rum

Fill a cocktail shaker with ice. Add first 7 ingredients. Shake well and strain into highball glass. Add additional ice cubes. Garnish with fruit. Pour Demerara rum over top.

TEQUILA

Here's a little true-and-false quiz Cliff and I worked up to test your tequila I.Q. The first person to get them all right gets a margarita.

1. Tequila was named for the first overweight Mexican bartender. *FALSE.* (The beverage was named after the town of Tequila in Mexico.)

2. Tequila is called the cactus whiskey because it is made from the sap of the aloe vera plant. *FALSE.* (It is made from the sap of the mescal plant, a very superior kind of Mexican cactus. And it takes about twelve to thirteen years to mature.)

3. Tequila tastes sweet and syrupy. *FALSE.* (Tequila is tart tasting and leaves a tingly sensation in the mouth.)

4. The great Aztec chief Montezuma believed tequila had the restorative properties of the fountain of youth. *TRUE.* (He did believe that tequila could restore health and vigor. And it was often used in rituals and ceremonies—I used to drink tequila

occasionally, which may be one reason for my own personal health and vigor.)

5. Tequila is traditionally taken straight by adding a pinch of salt and some lime juice to dilute the bitter taste. *FALSE.* (The way to drink tequila straight is to tilt your head back, squeeze a little lime juice in your mouth, followed by a pinch of salt. Then you down the shot of tequila in one gulp.)

Now for all you super brains, here's a bonus question:

6. If you drink a gallon of tequila within one hour and light a match, nothing will happen to you. *TRUE.* (You wouldn't be around to find the match!)

The following recipes serve one.

BLOODY MARIA

1 1/2 ounces light tequila
1 ounce tomato juice
1 tablespoon lemon juice
1 dash Worcestershire sauce
1 dash Tabasco
Salt and pepper to taste

Fill a cocktail shaker with ice. Add all ingredients and shake thoroughly. Strain into a sour or old-fashioned glass.

DORADO COCKTAIL

2 1/2 ounces dark tequila
1 tablespoon honey
2 tablespoons lemon

Fill a cocktail shaker with ice. Add all ingredients and shake vigorously. Strain into a cocktail glass.

EL DIABLO

2 ounces dark tequila
1/2 ounce crème de cassis
1 1/2 teaspoons lime juice
Sparkling mineral water
1 lime slice

Fill a tall glass with ice. Add first 3 ingredients, then mineral water, and stir gently. Garnish with lime.

MARGARITA

Cut lime
Salt
2 ounces dark tequila
1/2 ounce Cointreau
1 tablespoon lime juice
1 lime peel

Rub rim of the glass with lime. Then dip into salt. Fill a cocktail shaker with ice. Add ingredients and shake well. Strain into glass. Twist lime peel over drink and drop into glass. Serve in champagne glass.

PICADOR

2 ounces dark tequila
1 ounce Kahlúa
1 lime peel

Fill a mixing glass with crushed ice. Add tequila and Kahlúa and stir well. Strain into a cocktail glass. Twist peel over drink and drop into glass.

STRAWBERRY MARGARITA

2 ounces light tequila
1/2 ounce strawberry liqueur
1/2 cup sliced strawberries
1/2 ounce lime juice
1/2 teaspoon superfine sugar
1 fresh strawberry with stem

Fill an electric blender with all ingredients except strawberry with stem. Add 1/3 cup crushed ice and blend at low speed until smooth. Pour into a saucer champagne glass and garnish with strawberry.

TEQUILA COLADA

2 ounces light tequila
1 ounce cream of coconut
3 ounces pineapple juice
1 pineapple stick
1 lime slice

Fill an electric blender with first 3 ingredients. Add ⅓ cup crushed ice and blend at low speed until smooth. Pour into a tall glass filled with ice. Garnish with fruit.

TEQUILA COLLINS

1 tablespoon superfine sugar
2½ ounces lime juice
1½ ounces of light tequila
Club soda
1 orange slice
1 lemon slice
1 Maraschino cherry

Stir sugar and lime juice to dissolve. Add with tequila to an ice-filled cocktail mixer. Stir until well blended. Strain into a highball glass filled with ice. Add club soda. Garnish with fruit.

TEQUILA DRIVER

2 ounces light tequila
Orange juice
1 dash Perrier
1 orange slice

Fill a highball glass with ice. Add tequila. Fill to top with orange juice and stir gently. Sprinkle top with Perrier and garnish with fruit.

TEQUILA SOUR

2 ounces dark tequila
2½ ounces lemon juice
1 tablespoon superfine sugar

1/2 lemon slice
1 Maraschino cherry

Fill a cocktail shaker with ice. Add first 3 ingredients. Shake well and strain into a sour glass. Garnish with fruit.

TEQUILA SUNRISE
2 ounces dark tequila
4 ounces orange juice
3/4 ounce grenadine

Fill a mixing glass with ice. Add tequila and orange juice. Stir well. Strain into a highball glass filled with ice. Slowly pour grenadine over top and allow it to settle to bottom.

TEQUILA SUNSET
2 ounces light tequila
1 1/2 ounces lime juice
1/2 ounce grenadine
1 lime slice

Fill an electric blender with all ingredients except lime slice. Add 1/2 cup crushed ice and blend at low speed until smooth. Pour into old-fashioned glass filled with ice. Garnish with fruit.

TEQUINI
2 ounces light tequila
1/2 ounce dry vermouth
1 lemon peel

Fill a mixing glass with ice. Add tequila and vermouth and stir. Strain into a cocktail glass, twist peel over drink, and drop into glass.

TOREADOR
2 ounces light tequila
1/2 ounce white crème de cacao
1 tablespoon heavy cream
Whipped cream
Cocoa

Fill a cocktail shaker with ice. Add first 3 ingredients and shake thoroughly. Strain into a chilled cocktail glass. Garnish with whipped cream and dust with cocoa.

VIVA VILLA

2 ounces light tequila
2¹/₂ ounces lime juice
1 tablespoon superfine sugar
Salt

Fill a cocktail shaker with ice. Add all ingredients except salt and shake well. Pour into an ice-filled old-fashioned glass that has been rimmed with salt.

VODKA

Did you know that Polish vodka started out as a cold cure? Or that vodka was used by the Russians as a liniment? Or that vodka is made out of fermented grain mash and not mashed potatoes as some people think?

Today it's the number-one selling spirit around, accounting for about 30 percent of the liquor market. And that's pretty amazing because its popularity depends on being the most boring beverage you can imagine—sort of like Diane on a date.

Although vodka has no distinctive taste or smell of its own, I guess you'd have to call it the perfect drink, since it will mix well with almost anything. So, the next time you're in the mood for a little exotica, or just want to add some zip to your freshly squeezed orange juice, why not add a little vodka? Plain or fancy, sweet or sour, the sky's the limit on what you can make.

The following recipes make one serving each.

BLACK RUSSIAN

1½ ounces vodka
1½ ounces Kahlúa

Fill an old-fashioned glass with ice. Add ingredients and stir gently.

BLOODY BULL

1½ ounces vodka
3 ounces tomato juice
1½ ounces chilled beef bouillon
1 dash salt
1 dash each Worcestershire and
  Tabasco sauce

Fill a cocktail shaker with ice. Add all ingredients and mix well. Strain into a sour glass.

BLOODY MARY

1½ ounces vodka
3 ounces tomato juice
1 tablespoon lemon juice
1 dash each Worcestershire and
  Tabasco sauce
Salt and pepper
1 celery stalk

Fill a cocktail shaker with ice. Add all ingredients and mix thoroughly. Strain into a sour or old-fashioned glass filled with ice cubes. Garnish with vegetables of choice (celery stalk).

BUCKEYE

2¼ ounces vodka
¼ ounce dry vermouth
1 black olive

Fill a mixing glass with ice. Add vodka and vermouth and mix well until chilled. Strain into a chilled cocktail glass and garnish with olive.

VODKA BULLSHOT

2 ounces vodka
4 ounces chilled beef bouillon
Salt and pepper

Fill a mixing glass with ice. Add all ingredients and mix well. Strain into a large wineglass or an old-fashioned glass filled with ice.

CAPE CODDER

1½ ounces vodka
2 ounces cranberry juice

Fill a highball glass with ice. Add ingredients. Stir gently.

CLAMDIGGER

1½ ounces vodka
3 ounces clam juice
3 ounces tomato juice
1 dash Tabasco
1 celery rib
1 cherry tomato

Fill a highball glass with ice. Add first 4 ingredients and stir. Garnish with celery and cherry tomato.

COPPERHEAD

1 lime wedge
1½ ounces vodka
Ginger ale

Fill a highball glass with ice. Squeeze lime over it and drop into glass. Add vodka, fill glass to top with ginger ale, and stir gently.

FLYING GRASSHOPPER

1 ounce vodka
1/2 ounce white crème de menthe
1/2 ounce white crème de cacao

Fill a mixing glass with ice. Add all ingredients and shake well. Strain into a chilled cocktail glass.

GODMOTHER

1 1/2 ounces vodka
3/4 ounce amaretto
Orange juice

Fill an old-fashioned glass with ice. Add vodka and amaretto. Splash with orange juice.

GOLDEN SCREW

1 1/2 ounces vodka
3 ounces orange juice
1 dash angostura bitters

Fill a cocktail shaker with ice. Add all ingredients and shake thoroughly. Strain into a cocktail glass.

HARVEY WALLBANGER

1 ounce vodka
4 ounces orange juice
1/2 ounce Galliano

Fill a highball glass with ice. Add all ingredients and stir gently.

MOSCOW MULE

1/2 lime
2 ounces vodka
Ginger beer

Fill a 12-ounce glass with ice. Squeeze lime over ice and drop into glass. Add vodka and fill with ginger beer. Stir gently.

RUSSIAN BEAR

1 ounce vodka
1/2 ounce white crème de cacao
1/2 ounce heavy cream

Fill a cocktail shaker with ice. Add all ingredients and mix thoroughly. Strain into a chilled cocktail glass.

SALTY DOG

2 ounces vodka
4 ounces grapefruit juice
1 teaspoon lemon juice
Salt

Fill a cocktail shaker with ice. Add all ingredients except salt and mix well. Strain into a chilled cocktail glass and sprinkle top of drink with salt.

SCREWDRIVER

2 ounces vodka
Orange juice

Fill a highball glass with ice. Add vodka and orange juice and stir gently.

VODKA AND TONIC

1 lime wedge
2 ounces vodka
Quinine water

Fill a tall glass with ice. Squeeze lime over ice and drop into glass. Pour in vodka and fill glass to top with quinine water.

VODKA COLLINS

2 1/2 ounces vodka
1 1/2 teaspoons superfine sugar
1 ounce lime juice
Club soda
1 lemon slice

1 orange slice
1 Maraschino cherry

Fill a cocktail shaker with ice. Add first 3 ingredients. Strain into a collins glass half filled with ice. Add soda and stir gently. Garnish with fruit.

VODKA GIBSON

1/2–3/4 ounce dry vermouth
2–3 ounces vodka
1 cocktail onion

Fill a mixing glass with ice. Add vermouth and vodka and mix gently until well blended. Strain into a cocktail glass and garnish with onion.

VODKA GIMLET

1 1/2 ounces vodka
1/2 ounce Rose's lime juice
1 teaspoon superfine sugar

Fill a mixing glass wtih ice. Add all ingredients and shake well. Strain into a chilled cocktail glass.

VODKA MARTINI

2 1/2 ounces vodka
1/2 ounce dry vermouth
1 twist of lemon peel

Fill a mixing glass wtih ice. Add vodka and vermouth and shake well. Strain into a chilled cocktail glass. Garnish with lemon peel.

VODKA ON THE ROCKS

2 ounces vodka
1 twist of lemon peel

Fill an old-fashioned glass with ice. Pour in vodka. Add twist.

VODKA RICKEY

1 lime wedge
1½ ounces vodka
Sparkling mineral water

Fill a tall glass with ice. Squeeze lime juice over ice and drop into glass. Pour in vodka and fill glass to top with mineral water.

VODKA SLING

1 teaspoon superfine sugar
2 tablespoons lemon juice
2 ounces vodka
Plain or mineral water

Fill a highball glass with sugar and lemon juice and stir until dissolved. Add ice, vodka, and fill with water. Stir gently.

VODKA SOUR

1½ ounces vodka
2½ ounces lemon juice
1 tablespoon superfine sugar
1 lemon slice
1 Maraschino cherry

Fill cocktail glass with ice. Add first 3 ingredients and blend well. Strain into a chilled sour glass. Garnish with fruit.

VODKA STINGER

1½ ounces vodka
½ ounce white crème de menthe

Fill a cocktail shaker with ice. Add ingredients. Shake vigorously until well mixed and frothy. Strain into a chilled cocktail glass.

VOLGA BOATMAN

1½ ounces vodka
1½ ounces cherry brandy

1 1/2 ounces orange juice
1 Maraschino cherry

Fill a mixing glass with ice. Add all ingredients except cherry and stir until well blended. Strain into a chilled cocktail glass and garnish with Maraschino cherry.

WARSAW

1 1/2 ounces vodka
1/2 ounce blackberry brandy
1/2 ounce dry vermouth
1 teaspoon fresh lemon juice
1 lemon peel

Fill a cocktail shaker with ice. Add all ingredients except lemon peel. Shake vigorously until well blended and frothy. Strain into a chilled cocktail glass. Twist lemon peel over the drink and drop into glass, if desired.

YELLOW JACKET

1 ounce vodka
1 ounce Benedictine
4 ounces fresh orange juice
1/2 orange slice

Fill a cocktail shaker with ice. Add all ingredients except orange slice. Shake vigorously until well blended and frothy. Strain into a chilled cocktail glass. Garnish with orange slice.

ZEUS COCKTAIL

1 ounce vodka
2 ounces Campari
1 twist of lemon peel

Fill a mixing glass with ice. Add vodka and Campari. Stir until well mixed. Strain into a chilled cocktail glass and garnish with lemon peel.

WHISKEY

Whiskey has an absolutely fascinating history, which you probably don't want to hear, unless your hobby happens to be moonshining. So, I'll get right to the important facts.

The Irish claim to have invented it a thousand years ago, then brought it over to Scotland, where the Scots promptly adapted it for their own rather extensive use.

Although Scotch has a pretty big fan club today, nobody really drank the stuff until one hundred years ago when an American bug blight nearly wiped out all the European vineyards and put a temporary end to the brandy supply, the favored drink of the day.

Quick to recognize a good opportunity when they saw it, the Scots found that by cutting their drink with grain whiskey, sometimes as many as sixty-five different blends, they could get thirsty Americans to like it. So, I guess you could say we made Scotch what it is today.

All whiskeys are made from fermented grain mash, then aged in a barrel. It is measured by its proof, so a label reading "100 proof" means 50 percent alcohol. But from then on the choices do get interesting.

There are eight whiskeys made in the United States:

Blended. These are a combination of grain neutral spirits and straight whiskeys that have been blended together for a very distinctive flavor.

Bottled in bond. This is a straight whiskey, usually rye or bourbon, which gets its distinctive quality from the distillation process used.

Bourbon. This is a type of sour mash whiskey. To be called bourbon, it must be distilled at a proof no higher than 160; it must be aged in new charred barrels for at least two years; and it must contain 51 percent corn.

Corn. This whiskey, which has a slightly bitey taste, has to be made from 80 percent corn mash and aged in uncharred barrels.

Rye. This smooth-tasting whiskey must contain 51 percent rye at a distillate not exceeding 160 and aged in new charred oak barrels.

Sour mash. What makes the difference between this whiskey and the others is the type of yeast used in the fermenting process. It is also stronger and higher in proof.

Straight. This whiskey is like sour mash, but without as much kick. It can be made from rye, corn, wheat, or barley grains; distilled at no more than 160 proof; and aged seven years or more (two years minimum) in new charred oak barrels.

Tennessee. Very similar to bourbon in taste, the difference between these two whiskeys is in the distillation process.

Then we have some contributions from our neighbors in the North, East, and British Isles.

Canadian whiskey. Its most distinguishing feature is its light body and sweet taste.

Irish whiskey. This is blended, and it's the only whiskey in the world that's distilled three times, giving it a characteristically smooth, sweet taste.

Japanese. They make a Scotch called Sontory. It tastes light and smooth, but as of yet, hasn't developed a following like the more traditional brands.

Scotch. This is a blended whiskey with a distinctive smoky taste.

The following recipes make one serving each.

ALGONQUIN

1 1/2 ounces blended whiskey
1 ounce dry vermouth
1 ounce pineapple juice

Fill a cocktail shaker with ice. Add all ingredients and shake well. Pour into a cocktail glass.

BLARNEY STONE COCKTAIL

2 ounces Irish whiskey
1/2 teaspoon anisette
1/2 teaspoon Triple Sec
1/4 teaspoon Maraschino
1 dash angostura bitters
1 orange peel
1 green olive

Fill a cocktail shaker with ice. Add first 5 ingredients and blend well. Strain into a chilled cocktail glass. Twist orange peel over drink and drop into glass. Garnish with olive.

BLOOD AND SAND

1/2 ounce Scotch whiskey
1/2 ounce cherry brandy
1/2 ounce sweet vermouth
1/2 ounce orange juice

Fill a mixing glass with ice. Add all ingredients and stir well. Strain into a cocktail glass.

BOILERMAKER

1 1/2 ounces whiskey
Ice cold beer or ale

Fill a shot glass with whiskey. Pour beer into a chilled mug and serve separately.

BOURBON HIGHBALL

1 1/2 ounces bourbon
Water

Fill a highball glass with ice. Add bourbon and water and stir gently.

BOURBON MANHATTAN

2 1/2 ounces bourbon
1/2 ounce sweet vermouth

1 dash angostura bitters
1 Maraschino cherry

Fill a mixing glass with ice. Add all ingredients but cherry and stir. Strain into a cocktail glass and garnish with cherry.

BOURBON SOUR

1¹/₂ ounces bourbon
1¹/₂ ounces lemon juice
¹/₂ teaspoon superfine sugar
1 lemon slice
1 Maraschino cherry

Fill a cocktail shaker with ice. Add first 3 ingredients and mix well. Strain into a chilled sour glass and garnish with fruit.

COMMODORE

3 ounces blended whiskey
1 teaspoon lime juice
1 teaspoon orange juice
1 teaspoon strawberry liqueur
1 dash orange bitters
1 fresh strawberry with stem·

Fill a cocktail shaker with ice. Add all ingredients except strawberry and mix well. Strain into a chilled cocktail glass. Garnish with strawberry.

DRY MANHATTAN

2¹/₂ ounces blended whiskey
³/₄ ounce dry vermouth
1 dash angostura bitters
1 lemon peel

Fill a cocktail mixing glass with ice. Add all ingredients except lemon peel and stir. Strain into a chilled cocktail glass. Twist peel over drink and add to glass.

FINNEGAN'S WAKE

1 1/2 ounces Irish whiskey
1 1/2 ounces Irish Mist

Fill an old-fashioned glass with ice. Add ingredients. Stir gently.

GODFATHER

1 1/2 ounces Scotch
3/4 ounce amaretto

Fill an old-fashioned glass with ice. Add ingredients and stir gently.

HOLE-IN-ONE

1 3/4 ounces Scotch
3/4 ounce dry vermouth
1/4 teaspoon lemon juice
1 dash orange bitters

Fill a cocktail shaker with ice. Add all ingredients and mix well. Strain into a chilled cocktail glass.

IRISH RICKEY

1 lime wedge
1 1/2 ounces Irish whiskey
Sparkling mineral water

Fill a highball glass with ice. Squeeze lime wedge over ice and drop into glass. Add whiskey and water and stir gently.

IRISH SHILLELAGH

1 1/2 ounces Irish whiskey
1/2 ounce sloe gin
1/2 ounce light rum
2 tablespoons lemon juice
1 teaspoon superfine sugar
2 fresh peach slices
2 raspberries
1 strawberry
1 Maraschino cherry

Fill a cocktail shaker with first 5 ingredients and shake vigorously. Strain into a cocktail glass and garnish with fruit.

KENTUCKY
COCKTAIL

1 1/2 ounces bourbon
3/4 ounce pineapple juice

Fill a cocktail shaker with ice. Add ingredients and shake vigorously. Strain into a chilled cocktail glass.

MANHATTAN

2 1/2 ounces blended whiskey
1/2 ounce sweet vermouth
1 dash angostura bitters
1 Maraschino cherry

Fill a mixing glass with ice. Add all ingredients except cherry and shake well. Strain into a cocktail glass. Garnish with cherry.

NEW YORKER

1 1/2 ounces blended whiskey
1/2 ounce lime juice
1 teaspoon superfine sugar
1/4 teaspoon grenadine
1 lemon peel
1 orange peel

Fill a cocktail shaker with ice. Add first 4 ingredients and mix well. Wet the rim of a cocktail glass and dip into sugar. Strain ingredients into glass. Twist lemon and orange peels over drink and drop into glass.

OLD-FASHIONED

1 sugar cube
1 dash angostura bitters
1 teaspoon water
2–3 ounces blended whiskey
1 lemon peel
1 orange slice (optional)
1 Maraschino cherry

Fill an old-fashioned glass with sugar, bitters, and water. Stir until sugar dissolves. Add ice and whiskey and stir well. Twist lemon peel over glass and add to drink. Garnish with fruit.

PREAKNESS

1 1/2 ounces rye whiskey
1/2 ounce sweet vermouth
1/2 teaspoon Benedictine
1 dash angostura bitters
1 lemon peel

Fill a cocktail mixing glass with ice. Add all ingredients except lemon peel and stir well. Strain into a cocktail glass. Twist peel over glass and drop into drink.

PRESBYTERIAN

3 ounces bourbon
2 ounces ginger ale
2 ounces club soda
1 lemon peel

Fill a highball glass with ice. Add bourbon and mixers. Stir gently. Twist lemon peel over glass and add to drink.

ROB ROY

2 1/2 ounces Scotch
1/2 ounce sweet vermouth
1 Maraschino cherry
1 twist of lemon peel

Fill a cocktail shaker with ice. Add Scotch and vermouth and shake well. Garnish with fruit.

ROCK AND RYE

1 piece rock candy
3 ounces rye whiskey
1/2 teaspoon lemon juice

Dissolve the rock candy in the whiskey. Add lemon juice. Serve over ice in a cocktail glass.

SAZERAC

1 ounce Pernod
2 ounces bourbon or rye whiskey
¼ teaspoon Peychaud's bitters
½ teaspoon superfine sugar
1 lemon peel

Coat the inside of a prechilled old-fashioned glass with Pernod. Discard excess. Fill a cocktail mixing glass with ice. Add next 3 ingredients and stir until sugar is dissolved. Strain into the coated glass. Twist lemon peel over glass and add to drink.

SCOTCH HIGHBALL

1½ ounces Scotch
Water

Fill a highball glass with ice. Add Scotch and water. Stir gently

SCOTCH MIST

2 ounces Scotch
1 twist of lemon peel

Fill an old-fashioned glass with crushed ice and add Scotch. Garnish with lemon twist and serve with a straw.

SCOTCH ON THE ROCKS

2 ounces Scotch
1 twist of lemon peel
Water

Fill an old-fashioned glass with ice cubes. Pour in whiskey and drop in lemon peel. Add a little cold water.

SCOTCH SIDECAR

1½ ounces Scotch
¾ ounce Cointreau
¾ ounce lemon juice

Fill a cocktail shaker with ice. Add all ingredients and shake thoroughly. Strain into a cocktail glass.

SCOTCH SOUR

2 ounces Scotch
2 tablespoons lemon juice
1 teaspoon superfine sugar
1 orange slice
1 Maraschino cherry

Fill a cocktail shaker with ice. Add first 3 ingredients. Shake well. Strain into a sour glass. Garnish with fruit.

SERPENT'S TOOTH

1 ounce Irish whiskey
2 ounces sweet vermouth
2 ounces lemon juice
1/2 ounce kümmel
1 dash angostura bitters

Fill a cocktail mixing glass with ice. Add all ingredients and stir well. Strain into a cocktail glass.

SHAMROCK

1 ounce Irish whiskey
1 ounce dry vermouth
3 dashes green Chartreuse
3 dashes white crème de menthe
1 green olive

Fill a cocktail mixing glass with ice. Add all ingredients except olive and stir well. Strain into a cocktail glass. Add green olive.

SINGAPORE

1 1/2 ounces Canadian whiskey
1/4 ounce sloe gin
1/4 ounce Rose's Lime Juice
1/2 ounce lemon juice
1 cucumber peel

Fill a cocktail shaker with ice. Add all ingredients except cucumber peel and shake well. Strain into an old-fashioned glass filled with ice. Garnish with peel.

TIPPERARY

³/4 ounce Irish whiskey
³/4 ounce yellow Chartreuse
³/4 ounce sweet vermouth

Fill a cocktail mixing glass with ice. Add all ingredients and stir well. Strain into a cocktail glass.

T.N.T.

1 ounce blended whiskey
1 ounce anisette

Fill a cocktail shaker with ice. Add ingredients and mix well. Strain into a chilled cocktail glass.

TWIN HILLS

1¹/2 ounces blended whiskey
2 teaspoons Benedictine
1¹/2 teaspoons lemon juice
1¹/2 teaspoons lime juice
1 teaspoon superfine sugar
1 lemon slice
1 lime slice

Fill a cocktail shaker with ice. Add first 5 ingredients and mix vigorously. Strain into a chilled sour glass. Garnish with fruit.

WARD EIGHT

1¹/2 ounces blended whiskey
¹/2 ounce lemon juice
1 teaspoon superfine sugar
¹/2 teaspoon grenadine
1 lemon slice

Fill a cocktail shaker with ice. Add all ingredients except lemon slice and mix well. Strain into a tall glass filled with ice. Garnish with fruit.

WHISKEY HIGHBALL   1½ ounces whiskey
                        Water
                        1 lemon peel

Fill a highball glass with ice cubes. Add whiskey, then fill with water and stir gently. Twist peel over glass and add to drink.

WHISKEY SOUR   2 ounces blended whiskey
                        2½ ounces lemon juice
                        1 tablespoon superfine sugar
                        1 orange slice
                        1 Maraschino cherry

Fill a cocktail shaker with ice. Add first 3 ingredients and mix well. Strain into a sour glass. Garnish with fruit.

AFTERDINNER AND CREAM DRINKS

Don't get fooled into thinking that liqueurs are drinks with only snob appeal, though they do appeal to our Learned Waitress over here. There's nothing better to top off a good meal or give you that relaxing sigh of relief than an afterdinner or cream drink. Many people like these sweet, smooth-tasting beverages instead of dessert. And lately, afterdinner drinks are making their way into cocktail time, especially the cream concoctions, because they aren't alcoholically overpowering.

Hundreds of years ago, monks began experimenting with liqueurs for medicinal purposes. Today Chartreuse is the only one still produced by a religious order. Liqueurs have lasted, and there are hundreds on the market, offering a wide variety of tastes from plants, roots, herbs, and flowers, to fruits and seeds, which are distilled or mixed with spirits and sweetened. Each liqueur is different from the next, due to the unique combination of ingredients that go into each kind. Sometimes as many as several hundred items go into one liqueur.

If you really want to test out your bartending skills and create a spectacular and delicious taste treat, try floating a liqueur. Because the densities are different, you can create your own rainbows, as long as you remember to use the ingredients in the order in which they are given, and to follow the directions.

See the Glossary for a complete list of leading liqueurs. The following recipes each make one serving.

A AND B

$^1/_2$ ounce Benedictine
$^1/_2$ ounce applejack

Pour the Benedictine, then the applejack into a straight-sided liqueur glass so that applejack floats on top of Benedictine.

AMARETTO

$1^1/_2$ ounces amaretto
$^3/_4$ ounce white crème de menthe

Fill a cocktail shaker with ice. Add ingredients. Shake vigorously and strain into a chilled cocktail glass.

AMARETTO AND CREAM

$1^1/_2$ ounces amaretto
$1^1/_2$ ounces heavy cream

Fill a cocktail shaker with ice. Add ingredients. Shake vigorously and strain into a chilled cocktail glass.

ANGEL'S TOUCH

¹/₄ ounce white crème de cacao
¹/₄ ounce crème de cassis
¹/₄ ounce heavy cream

Pour the ingredients, as listed, into a straight-sided liqueur glass. As you pour make sure that each ingredient floats on top of the other.

BRANDY ALEXANDER

¹/₂ ounce brandy
¹/₂ ounce brown crème de cacao
2 ounces heavy cream
Nutmeg

Fill a cocktail blender with ice. Add all ingredients except nutmeg and mix well. Strain into a chilled cocktail glass. Garnish with nutmeg.

BRANDY MIST

2¹/₂ ounces Metaxa
Splash of water

Fill an old-fashioned glass with ¹/₂ cup crushed ice. Pour brandy over ice and serve with a straw.

COFFEE GRASSHOPPER

³/₄ ounce coffee liqueur
³/₄ ounce white crème de menthe
1 ounce heavy cream

Fill a cocktail shaker with ice. Add all ingredients and shake vigorously. Strain into a chilled cocktail glass.

GOLDEN CADILLAC

³/₄ ounce white crème de cacao
³/₄ ounce Galliano
³/₄ ounce heavy cream

Fill an electric blender with all ingredients. Add ⅓ cup crushed ice. Blend at low speed until smooth. Pour into a saucer champagne glass.

GRASSHOPPER

¾ ounce white crème de cacao
¾ ounce green crème de menthe
¾ ounce heavy cream

Fill a cocktail shaker with ice. Add all ingredients, shake vigorously, and strain into a chilled cocktail glass.

GREEN DRAGON

1 ounce green crème de menthe
1½ ounces vodka

Fill a cocktail mixing glass with ingredients and stir well. Then pour into a saucer champagne glass packed with crushed ice.

MOCHA MINT

¾ ounce coffee liqueur
¾ ounce white crème de menthe
¾ ounce white crème de cacao

Fill a cocktail shaker with ice. Add all ingredients and shake thoroughly. Strain into a sugar-frosted cocktail glass.

PINK SQUIRREL

1 ounce crème de noyau
1 ounce white crème de cacao
¾ ounce heavy cream

Fill a cocktail shaker with ice. Add all ingredients and shake vigorously. Strain into a chilled, sugar-frosted cocktail glass.

PRINCESS

2 ounces apricot brandy
½ ounce heavy cream

Pour the apricot brandy into a large liqueur glass. Carefully add heavy cream so that it floats on top.

RUSSIAN COFFEE

³/4 ounce coffee liqueur
³/4 ounce vodka
³/4 ounce heavy cream

Fill an electric blender with all ingredients. Add ¹/3 cup of crushed ice and blend at low speed until smooth. Pour into a saucer champagne glass.

RUSTY NAIL

1¹/2 ounces Scotch
1¹/2 ounces Drambuie

Fill an old-fashioned glass with ice. Add ingredients and stir gently.

COFFEE DRINKS

Coffee drinks are in a class by themselves. Piping hot and laced with your favorite brandy, liqueur, or spirits, they're a great way to end any meal. You can make them as fancy as the Café Royale and Café Diable (see recipes) or as simple as the old standby, Irish Coffee. No matter what you decide, you'll impress your guests, and have a deliciously warm drink.

Each of these recipes makes one serving, unless otherwise indicated.

CAFÉ AU COGNAC

1 lemon wedge
1 teaspoon superfine sugar
4 ounces hot coffee
1 ounce brandy

Rub the rim of a 6-ounce goblet with lemon. Then dip in sugar. Fill glass ¾ full with coffee and float brandy on top. Light brandy on top and serve.

CAFÉ AU KIRSCH

1 ounce kirsch
1 ounce cold black coffee
½ teaspoon superfine sugar
1 egg white

Fill an electric blender with all ingredients. Add 1 cup cracked ice and blend at high speed until smooth. Pour into a chilled cocktail glass.

CAFÉ BRÛLOT

9 ounces brandy
6 sugar cubes
1 twist of lemon peel
2 twists of orange peel
2 cinnamon sticks, halved
12 whole cloves
12 ounces hot coffee

Slowly heat all ingredients except coffee in a chafing dish. Then light mixture and let it flame for a minute. Slowly pour in coffee, and stir gently. Makes 6 demitasse servings.

CAFÉ DIABLE

4 ounces dark rum
2 cinnamon sticks, halved
2 tablespoons superfine sugar
Zest of 2 oranges stuck with cloves
6 cups hot coffee

Slowly heat all ingredients except coffee in a chafing dish. Then light mixture and let it flame for a minute. Slowly pour in coffee, and stir gently. Makes 6 mug-sized servings.

CAFÉ PUCCI

1 ounce golden rum
1 ounce amaretto
5 ounces hot coffee
1 tablespoon whipped cream

Fill an 8-ounce mug with rum and amaretto. Add coffee. Stir gently. Top with cream.

CAFÉ ROYALE

4 ounces hot coffee
1 1/2 ounces brandy
1 sugar cube

Fill a demitasse cup with coffee. Pour brandy in a teaspoon, and hold it over the cup. Place sugar cube in brandy and ignite it, dropping contents of spoon in the cup when the flame dies.

CAFÉ ROYALE FRAPPE

Superfine sugar to taste
2 ounces cold black coffee
1 ounce brandy

Sweeten coffee. Fill a cocktail shaker with 1/2 cup crushed ice and add ingredients. Shake thoroughly. Pour into a chilled saucer champagne glass. Serve with a straw.

COFFEE WITH COGNAC

1 lemon peel
Superfine sugar
4 ounces hot coffee
1 ounce cognac

Coat the rim of a demitasse cup with lemon peel and frost with sugar. Fill with hot coffee and float brandy on top. Ignite brandy and serve.

DUTCH COFFEE

2 ounces Vandermint liqueur
5 ounces hot coffee
1 tablespoon whipped cream
Cocoa

Fill a coffee mug with liqueur and coffee and stir gently. Top with whipped cream and dust with cocoa.

IRISH COFFEE

1 1/2 ounces Irish whiskey
5 ounces hot coffee
1 teaspoon superfine sugar
1 tablespoon whipped cream

Fill a warmed 8-ounce goblet with whiskey, coffee, and sugar. Stir gently until sugar is dissolved. Top with cream.

JAMAICAN COFFEE

1 ounce Tia Maria
3/4 ounce light rum
5 ounces hot coffee
1 tablespoon whipped cream
Nutmeg

Fill a warmed 8-ounce goblet with first 3 ingredients and stir gently. Top with cream and dust lightly with nutmeg.

KAHLÚA COFFEE

1 1/2 ounces Kahlúa
5 ounces hot, strong coffee
1 tablespoon whipped cream
Cinnamon

Fill a warmed 8-ounce goblet with Kahlúa and coffee. Stir gently, top with whipped cream, and sprinkle cinnamon on top.

MEXICAN COFFEE

³/4 ounce brandy
³/4 ounce Kahlúa
5 ounces hot coffee
1 tablespoon whipped cream

Fill a warmed 8-ounce goblet with brandy, Kahlúa, and coffee. Stir gently. Top with cream.

MOCHA RUM

1¹/2 ounces rum
3 ounces hot coffee
3 ounces hot cocoa
1 teaspoon superfine sugar
2 tablespoons whipped cream

Fill a coffee mug with all ingredients except cream. Stir gently. Top with whipped cream.

VESUVIO

4 ounces strong, hot coffee
1 sugar cube
1 ounce Sambuca
1 lemon peel

Fill a demitasse cup with hot coffee. Add sugar cube and stir to dissolve sugar completely. Add Sambuca. Twist lemon peel over drink and drop into glass.

PUNCHES AND EGGNOGS

Punches are mistake proof. Eggnogs take a little more time and trouble to make. But either of these party favorites are such crowd pleasers, your skills as a mixologist are bound to be appreciated.

Don't underestimate the power of their potency though . . . some are guaranteed to break your lease. And as for the hot drinks, like Wassail, included in this section, you can also turn them into terrific punches. By simply multiplying the ingredients by the number of people you're expecting—whether it's one or one hundred—you'll be in business!

CASSIS PUNCH

2 cups whole strawberries
4 ounces crème de cassis
3 bottles sweet white wine

Soak strawberries in cassis for an hour or so. Strain. Add cassis and wine to punch bowl with block of ice. Float strawberries on top. Makes 20 4-ounce servings.

CHAMPAGNE PUNCH

28 ounces lemon juice
1 cup superfine sugar
16 ounces brandy
16 ounces orange curacao
64 ounces chilled champagne
32 ounces chilled ginger ale
1/2 pint Maraschino
Whole fresh strawberries

Stir lemon juice into sugar until dissolved. Add to punch bowl with block of ice and next 5 ingredients. Garnish with strawberries. Makes 40 4-ounce servings.

CHEERS ARTILLERY PUNCH

32 ounces bourbon
16 ounces light rum
8 ounces gin
8 ounces brandy
8 ounces Benedictine
8 ounces dark rum
16 ounces orange juice
8 ounces lemon juice
32 ounces black tea
1 bottle dry white wine
Twists of lemon peel
Twists of orange peel

Mix all ingredients except citrus peels in a large punch bowl with a block of ice. Garnish with lemon and orange peel twists. Makes 36 4-ounce servings.

CLARET PUNCH

1 cup superfine sugar
28 ounces lemon juice
96 ounces claret
8 ounces orange curaçao
16 ounces brandy
32 ounces mineral water
Fruit in season

Stir sugar into lemon juice until dissolved. Then add next 4 ingredients in punch bowl containing block of ice. Stir gently. Garnish with fruit. Makes 46 4-ounce servings.

GLOGG

1 bottle tawny port
1/2 bottle Madeira
1 bottle medium-dry sherry
1/2 bottle dry red wine
1 cinnamon stick
25 cloves
15 cardamom seeds
1 1/2 pounds sugar cubes
4 ounces brandy
1 cup raisins
1 cup blanched almonds

Heat first 7 ingredients in a heavy saucepan. When wine mixture is hot, place a rack on top of saucepan so that it covers half of it. Then arrange sugar cubes on rack, warm the brandy, pour over sugar mixture, and ignite. Ladle wine mixture over sugar mixture until it dissolves. Then add raisins and almonds, stir well. Makes 10 8-ounce servings.

HOT BUTTERED APPLEJACK

32 ounces sweet cider
4 teaspoons superfine sugar
Nutmeg
4 twists of lemon peel
4 cinnamon sticks
4 ounces applejack
4 pats butter

Heat cider to boiling point. Set out 4 10-ounce mugs. In each one, place 1 teaspoon sugar, dash nutmeg, twist of lemon peel, a cinnamon stick, and 1 ounce applejack. Fill with cider. Top with pat of butter. Serves 4.

**SANGRIA
CALIFORNIA STYLE**

1 cup superfine sugar
2 cups lemon juice
128 ounces California Zinfandel
8 ounces brandy
4 ounces Cointreau
64 ounces club soda
64 ounces orange juice
16 ounces lemon juice
3 oranges, sliced thin
3 lemons, sliced thin

Chill all ingredients. Stir sugar into lemon juice until dissolved. Add to remaining ingredients in a punch bowl with 12 ice cubes. Makes 100 4-ounce servings.

SUMMER PUNCH

3 bottles dry white wine
12 ounces crème de cassis
12 oranges, sliced
1 pint strawberries

Put all ingredients except strawberries into a punch bowl containing a block of ice and stir gently. Garnish with fruit. Makes 20 4-ounce servings.

VODKA PUNCH

1 bottle vodka
2 bottles champagne
Lemon slices
Fruit in season

Chill vodka and champagne. Pour into thoroughly chilled punch bowl. Garnish with fruit. Makes 18 4-ounce servings.

WASSAIL

15 small apples
15 teaspoons brown sugar
2 bottles dry sherry
1/2 teaspoon grated nutmeg
2 cups superfine sugar
6 eggs, separated
1 teaspoon ground ginger
3 whole cloves
1/2 teaspoon allspice
1 cinnamon stick
4 ounces water
8 ounces brandy

Core apples and fill each with 1 teaspoon brown sugar. Bake in oven at 350°F for 30 minutes or until tender, making sure to cover the bottom of the pan with 1/8" water. In a saucepan combine next 7 ingredients and heat on a low flame. Beat egg yolks until light and lemon colored. Beat whites until stiff and fold into yolks. Strain wine mixture and gradually add to eggs, stirring it constantly. Finally, add brandy and float apples on top. Makes 10 8-ounce servings.

WHISKEY PUNCH

12 ounces lemon juice
36 ounces orange juice
2 sugar cubes
1 1/2 bottles bourbon
3 ounces orange curaçao
64 ounces club soda
Fruits in season

Combine orange and lemon juice and stir in sugar until dissolved. Then combine with next 3 ingredients in punch bowl containing block of ice. Stir gently. Garnish with fruit. Makes 35 4-ounce servings.

BALTIMORE EGGNOG

12 eggs, separated
2 cups superfine sugar
16 ounces brandy
8 ounces light rum
8 ounces peach brandy
48 ounces milk
16 ounces heavy cream
Nutmeg

Beat egg yolks and sugar until thick. Slowly add brandy, rum, peach brandy, milk, and cream. Refrigerate until thoroughly chilled and pour into a punch bowl. Beat egg whites until still and fold carefully into eggnog. Sprinkle nutmeg on top. Makes 25 4-ounce servings.

BOURBON EGGNOG

12 eggs, separated
1 1/2 cups superfine sugar
32 ounces heavy cream
32 ounces milk
1 tablespoon vanilla
32 ounces bourbon
Nutmeg

Beat egg yolks with sugar until thick. Set container in middle of a large bowl filled with cracked ice. In a separate container, beat cream until stiff, add milk, vanilla, and stir in bourbon. Combine both mixtures in punch bowl. Beat egg whites until stiff and gently add them to eggnog mixture. Sprinkle nutmeg on top. Makes 25 4-ounce servings.

INSTANT EGGNOG

2 quarts vanilla ice cream
1 bottle bourbon
4 ounces light rum
Nutmeg

Put the ice cream in a punch bowl. Stir in bourbon and rum until thoroughly blended. Sprinkle nutmeg on top. Makes 25 4-ounce servings.

TOM AND JERRY

1 egg, separated
1 teaspoon superfine sugar
1¹/₂ ounces brandy
1¹/₂ ounces dark rum
6 ounces hot milk
Nutmeg

Beat egg white until it is stiff; beat yolk until it is thick and lemon colored. Combine white and yolk with sugar, then add with brandy and rum to a warmed 8-ounce mug. Fill to top with hot milk. Sprinkle with nutmeg. Serves 1.

HOT DRINKS

These recipes make one serving each.

BLUE BLAZER

3 ounces Scotch
3 ounces boiling water
1 teaspoon superfine sugar
1 twist of lemon peel

Fill a mug with Scotch and another one with boiling water. Ignite whiskey and while it is flaming, pour it and the water back and forth from one mug to another. Add sugar and serve with lemon peel in a warmed mug.

GROG

2 ounces dark rum
1 cube sugar
3 whole cloves
1 1-inch piece cinnamon stick
1 tablespoon lemon juice
1 lemon slice

Fill a mug with all ingredients. Stir to dissolve sugar, leaving the spoon in the mug. Then add boiling water to fill, and stir.

HOT BUTTERED RUM II

3 ounces dark rum
1 twist of lemon peel
1 cinnamon stick
4 whole cloves
Apple cider
1 tablespoon butter
Nutmeg

Put first 4 ingredients into a warmed 12-ounce mug. Heat cider to boiling and add to mixture. Top with a pat of butter and sprinkle with cinnamon.

MULLED WINE

8 ounces dry red wine
1 dash angostura bitters
3 whole cloves
1 pinch allspice
1 cinnamon stick
1 twist of lemon peel
1 teaspoon superfine sugar

Combine all ingredients in a small saucepan and heat, but not to boiling. Strain into an 8-ounce mug.

DRINKS OF THE CHEERS™ STARS*

And here they are. Each recipe makes one drink.

CARLA'S "LEAP INTO AN OPEN GRAVE"

¹/₂ ounce gin
1 ounce Cointreau
1 ounce Midori
¹/₂ ounce Rose's lime juice
Splash of champagne

Fill a blender with ice. Add all ingredients except champagne and blend well. Fill a tall glass with ice. Pour in mixture. Top with a splash of champagne.

*All the drinks were created especially for the Cheers stars by Dave Crocker and Ed Doyle at the Bull and Finch Pub.

CLIFF'S WINGO

1 ounce vodka
1¹/₂ ounce Midori
2 ounces milk

Fill an old-fashioned glass with ice. Add ingredients and stir gently.

COACH'S NONALCOHOLIC "RELIEF PITCHER"

1 ounce lemon juice
2 ounces orange juice
1 ounce cranberry juice
Splash of ginger ale

Fill a tall glass with ice. Add all juices and stir to blend. Top with a splash of ginger ale.

DIANE CHAMBERS' "SMASH"

1¹/₂ ounces vodka
¹/₂ ounce Triple Sec
3 ounces orange juice
Maraschino cherry

Fill an old-fashioned glass with ice. Add all ingredients except cherry. Stir gently. Garnish with cherry.

NORM'S BEST BEER

Any beer that produces at least a 1-inch head when poured with a steady hand from a height of 2 inches above the glass.

SAM MALONE'S "POOR YORICK"

¹/₄ ounce Triple Sec
2 ounces lemon juice
1 ounce orange juice
1 ounce light rum
¹/₄ ounce dark rum
Splash of club soda

Fill a cocktail shaker with ice. Add first 4 ingredients and blend well. Pour into a tall glass filled with ice. Float dark rum on top. Splash with club soda.

3

DIANE'S LOW-CAL DRINKS

If anyone ever tries to tell you that waitressing and staying slim at the same time is easy, you can politely inform them that their cranial cavity is filled with a finely ground organic woody substance—better known as sawdust.

Among the day-to-day charms of leading the life of a mobile purveyor of alcoholic beverages, there are a few unfortunate side effects. Apart from the obvious temptations to imbibe some extremely fattening concoctions, there is also a type of man who attempts to secure my charms with offers of romantic (fattening) candlelit dinners.

Being the sybaritic little featherweight that I am, there's the constant emotional battle of turning down these promises of gastronomical decadence and bacchanalian lust, or learning to live with a life of unwanted excess human tonnage.

As I am from the school of serious self-control, I manage to muster up enough psychological savvy to tell myself I should eat and drink with extreme caution, and, if I need further inducement, I merely look at what overindulgence has done to poor dear Carla. So, even while eating and drinking and making merry, I remember to count my calories. And you dieters who are drinkers, and drinkers who are watching your health and weight, can do the same.

As an ex-teaching assistant turned barperson, it didn't take very much of my academic logic to come up with a simple solution to the problem. Put away your pocket calculators, fellow imbibers, and follow me into the world of low-calorie drinkables.

Lesson number one is to know that most mixed drinks average about 176 calories for about every two ounces of liquor. By eliminating one ounce, you'll still have a fine-tasting drink, but you will save up to 100 calories per drink, depending on the beverage.

Just so that you will know how many hidden calories there are in your favorite drink, I've also included my informative, handy-dandy Calorie I.Q. chart, which you can use when making up your own low-cal combinations. Or you can switch to one of my specially selected recipes, which have already been de-calorized to take the guesswork out of slim-drinking.

Although it is difficult to give a specific calorie count after each drink, as this depends on the type of alcohol used as well as whether sweeteners used are low-cal, no-cal, or regular, you can expect to take onboard 40 to 80 calories for the wine-based cocktails, and about 100 for the spirit drinks. Each low-cal recipe serves one unless otherwise indicated.

APPLE RUM COOLER

³/4 ounce applejack
³/4 ounce light rum
Club soda
1 lime wedge
1 orange peel

Fill a tall glass with ice and add applejack and rum. Squeeze lime over drink and drop inside glass. Add club soda and garnish with orange peel.

BLACKBERRY COOLER

2 ounces blackberry brandy
2 dashes grenadine
Ginger ale
1 twist of lemon peel

Fill a tall glass with ice and add blackberry brandy and grenadine. Stir gently, then add ginger ale. Garnish with lemon peel.

BOCCIE BALL

1¹/2 ounces amaretto
1¹/2 ounces orange juice
2 ounces water

Fill a highball glass with all ingredients and stir gently.

BRANDY LOW-CAL

1 ounce brandy
Splash of club soda

Fill an old-fashioned glass with ice. Pour brandy over rocks and douse with club soda.

BYRRH CASSIS COOLER

2 ounces Byrrh
¹/2 ounce crème de cassis
Water
1 twist of lemon peel

Fill a tall glass with ice. Add Byrrh, crème de cassis, and enough water to fill glass. Stir gently.

CAMPARI SODA
1 1/2 ounces Campari
Splash of water
1 twist of lemon peel

Fill an old-fashioned glass with ice. Add Campari and a splash of water. Garnish with lemon twist.

CHAMPAGNE COOLER
1 ounce brandy
1 ounce Cointreau
6 ounces chilled champagne
1 fresh mint sprig

Fill a highball glass with ice. Add liquid ingredients. Garnish with mint.

CHARTREUSE COOLER
1 ounce yellow Chartreuse
3 ounces orange juice
1 ounce lime juice
Bitter lemon
1 orange slice

Pour first 3 ingredients into a cocktail shaker. Add bitter lemon to top of shaker. Shake well and pour into a tall glass filled with ice. Garnish with orange slice.

CLARET COOLER
4 ounces dry red wine
1/2 ounce brandy
1 ounce orange juice
3 ounces water
1/2 ounce lemon juice
1 lemon slice

Fill a tall glass with ice. Add all ingredients except lemon slice and stir gently. Garnish with fruit.

COFFEE CUP COOLER

4 ounces cold, black coffee
1 ounce vodka
1 ounce coffee liqueur
1 teaspoon superfine sugar
1 tablespoon whipped cream

Fill a cocktail shaker with ice. Add all ingredients, except cream. Shake well and pour into a tall glass filled with ice. Add whipped cream.

CRANBERRY COOLER

2 ounces cranberry liqueur
Club soda
1 orange slice

Fill a tall glass with ice. Add liqueur and club soda and stir gently. Garnish with fruit.

CURAÇAO COOLER

1 ounce blue curaçao
1 ounce vodka
1/2 ounce lime juice
1/2 ounce lemon juice
Splash of orange juice

Fill a cocktail shaker with ice. Add all ingredients except orange juice and blend. Pour into a tall glass filled with ice, add the orange juice, and stir gently.

DRY MANHATTAN COOLER

1 1/2 ounces blended whiskey
1 ounce dry vermouth
2 ounces orange juice
1/2 ounce lemon juice
1/2 ounce orgeat
Splash of water

Fill a cocktail shaker with all ingredients except water and blend well. Pour into a tall glass filled with ice. Add a splash of water and stir gently.

DRY VERMOUTH COOLER

2 ounces dry vermouth
1 twist of lemon peel

Fill an old-fashioned glass with ice. Add vermouth and garnish with lemon twist.

DUBONNET COOLER

1¹/₂ ounces Dubonnet Red
1¹/₂ ounces Dubonnet Blonde
Splash of water
1 lime wedge

Fill a tall glass with ice. Add Dubonnet and water and stir gently. Squeeze lime wedge into drink and drop into glass.

DUBONNET TEASER

1¹/₂ ounces Dubonnet
1 ounce gin
¹/₂ ounce cherry liqueur
¹/₂ ounce lemon juice
1 teaspoon superfine sugar
Club soda

Fill a cocktail shaker with ice. Add all ingredients except club soda and blend well. Pour into a tall glass filled with ice. Splash soda over drink and stir gently.

FLAVORED WHITE WINE

2 ounces dry white wine
Splash of orange juice

Fill an old-fashioned glass with ice. Add ingredients. Stir gently.

FLORADORA

2 ounces gin
3 tablespoons lime juice
1/2 teaspoon superfine sugar
1 tablespoon raspberry syrup
2 ounces ginger ale

Fill a tall glass with ice. Add all ingredients and stir gently.

GIN LOW-CAL

1/2 ounce gin
Splash of soda

Fill an old-fashioned glass with ice. Add ingredients and stir gently. (Scotch, bourbon, or vodka can be substituted for gin, if desired.)

HARVARD COOLER

2 ounces applejack
1/2 teaspoon superfine sugar
Club soda
1 orange peel

Fill a tall glass with ice. Add applejack and sugar and stir to dissolve sugar. Then splash with club soda and garnish with orange peel.

HIGHLAND COOLER

2 ounces Scotch
2 dashes angostura bitters
2 tablespoons lemon juice
1 teaspoon superfine sugar
Splash of ginger ale

Fill a tall glass with ice. Add all ingredients except ginger ale and stir. Splash with ginger ale.

LILLET-LIKE

2 ounces dry white wine
Squirt of seltzer
Splash of orange juice

Fill an old-fashioned glass with ice. Add wine and seltzer and splash of orange juice. Stir gently.

MANHATTAN COOLER

4 ounces dry red wine
3 dashes rum
1 1/2 teaspoons superfine sugar
2 tablespoons lemon juice
1 lemon slice

Fill a tall glass with ice. Add all ingredients except lemon and stir gently. Garnish with lemon slice.

NEGRONI COOLER

1 1/2 ounces Campari
1 1/2 ounces sweet vermouth
1 1/2 ounces gin
Splash of water
1 orange slice

Fill a mixing glass with first 3 ingredients. Blend well and pour into a tall glass filled with ice. Add a splash of water. Stir gently. Garnish with fruit.

PEAR IN WINE

1 pear, peeled
4 ounces white wine

Soak pear in wine. After it has had a chance to set for a while, drink the wine. Then eat the pear later for dessert.

PINEAPPLE MINT COOLER

1/2 ounce white crème de menthe
2 ounces gin
3 ounces pineapple juice
1 ounce lemon juice
Splash of water
1 pineapple spear

Fill a cocktail shaker with ice. Add first 4 ingredients and blend well. Pour into a tall glass filled with ice. Add splash water. Stir gently. Garnish with fruit.

ST. RAPHAEL COOLER

1/2 ounce St. Raphael
1 1/2 ounces gin
1 teaspoon superfine sugar
1/2 ounce lemon juice
Splash of water
1 lemon peel

Fill a mixing glass with ice. Add first 4 ingredients and blend well. Pour into a tall glass filled with ice. Splash with water. Twist lemon peel over drink and drop into glass.

REFRESHING ALCOHOLIC ICED TEA

12 tea bags
4 cups boiling water
Sugar to taste
2/3 cup lemon juice
3 cups dry white wine

Add tea bags to boiling water. Let stand for 5 minutes, then remove. Add sugar to taste. Let cool. Then add lemon juice and wine. Pour into a tall pitcher filled with ice. Serves 10 to 12.

RHINE WINE SPRITZER

4 ounces sweet white wine
Water
1 twist of lemon

Fill a tall glass with ice. Add wine and water and stir gently. Garnish with lemon.

ROCK AND RYE COOLER

1 ounce rock and rye
1 1/2 ounces vodka
Bitter lemon
1/2 ounce lime juice
1 lime slice

Fill a cocktail shaker with ice. Add first 2 ingredients, then bitter lemon to top of shaker, and blend. Pour into a tall glass filled with ice. Splash with lime juice. Garnish with lime slice.

RUM HIGHBALL

8 ounces iced tea
2 ounces rum
Sugar to taste
1 lemon slice

Fill a tall glass with ice. Add tea, rum, and sugar. Garnish with lemon slice.

TOMATO VERMOUTH

2 ounces dry vermouth
4 ounces tomato juice
1 twist of lemon

Fill an old-fashioned glass with ice. Add vermouth and juice. Stir gently. Garnish with lemon.

VERMOUTH COOLER

2 ounces dry vermouth
Splash of water
2 tablespoons raspberry syrup
1 orange slice

Fill a tall glass with ice. Add vermouth, water, and syrup. Stir gently to mix. Garnish with orange slice.

WHITE CLOUD

1 ounce Sambuca or anisette
Club soda
1 lime slice

Fill a tall glass with ice. Add anisette and club soda and stir gently. Garnish with lime slice.

WINE COOLER

4 ounces red or white wine
2 teaspoons superfine sugar
Splash of water
1 tablespoon orange juice
1 lemon or orange slice

Fill a tall glass with ice. Add all ingredients except fruit. Stir gently to dissolve sugar. Garnish red wine cooler with lemon, white wine cooler with orange slice.

Calorie I.Q.

Drinks	Calories per Ounce
Amaretto	110
Anisette	111
Beer (American)	16
Beer (imported)	18
Beer (near)	6
Benedictine	111
Bourbon	*
Brandy	75
Byrrh	24
Campari	28
Cassis	83
Champagne	20
Chartreuse (green)	100
Chartreuse (yellow)	125
Cognac	*
Cointreau	80
Crème de menthe	104
Curaçao	105
Daiquiri cocktail	190
Drambuie	110
Dubonnet	25
Gin	*
Kirsch	77
Martini (very dry), most other cocktails	60
Port	50
Rum	*

*The amount of calories per ounce is the same as the proof. For example, an ounce of 100-proof alcohol contains 100 calories.

Drinks	Calories per Ounce
Scotch	*
Sherry (dry)	40
St. Raphael	25
Table wines (most dry vintages)	20
Tom Collins	40
Vermouth (dry)	24
Vermouth (sweet)	45
Vodka	*

Mixers	Calories per Ounce
Club soda	0
Colas	6
Ginger ale	10
Grapefruit juice	10
Grape juice	12
Grenadine	25
Lemon juice	6
Lime juice	4
Orange juice	15
Orgeat syrup	103
Pineapple juice (unsweetened)	17
Sugar (1 teaspoon)	16
Tomato juice	3
Tonic water (quinine)	12
Water	0

4

CARLA'S HANGOVER HELPERS

Any bimboette can put a guy to bed once he's really polluted, but it takes a true princess to bring him kicking back to life again. I know, I've risen more bodies from the dead than the big man upstairs. You don't need a miracle to do it, just good old-fashioned know-how and a few tricks of the bar trade.

I've seen some of the biggest and strongest hunks in my life climb walls at the first sound of an Alka-Seltzer fizzing away in a glass, so the first thing you don't do is holler at them, as good as that might make you feel, unless, of course, you joined in the festivities yourself!

Face it, there's only one sure way to prevent a hangover—stomp on it before it starts. This doesn't mean missing out on a lot of whoopee, it just means taking precautions, watching your intake, and not making a fool of yourself.

For any of you uninitiated out there who've never suffered the ravages of a hangover, here's a brief description. (For those of you who actually fooled yourselves into believing it might have been "just something you ate," then this is just a cruel reminder.)

First of all, you've got birdcage breath, your mouth feels scummy, you have itchy teeth, and your tongue has grown hair. Then you notice the team of ballpark pros in your head, all hammering away with full-blown home runs and little bunts at the same time. When you open your eyes you find the light sets them off on a World Series winning streak. Some poor slobs even feel that their chests are first course on the barbecue grill, and the old love pump sounds like the drum corps of a marching band.

But there's worse to come . . . the time to throw up, or even more distressing, when you want to and can't. Great hangover experts can also suffer uncontrollable tremors, flushes and chills, acute depression, and all this while they watch invisible rats run up walls.

That's a full-blown hangover, and let's face it, who needs it?

WHAT CAUSES A HANGOVER?

If you really want to get blottoed, you should understand how it happens and why you feel like a slimebucket the next day. As well as getting you sloshed, booze also leads to some very complicated chemical changes in the body. After it has gotten into the blood through your stomach, it gets pumped up to the brain and begins to work on numbing brain cells. This is when you feel nice and dipsy and relaxed.

But as greater concentrations of alcohol build up, areas that control motor function become paralyzed, and that's when you start to lose your legs. Your speech becomes slurred, muscle control starts to disappear, and eventually you are about as much fun as a bowl of Jell-O, or Diane on her good days. You won't know much of what happens next, and it's probably just as well. What follows next is a stupor and then it's pass-out time. This sudden, usually unwanted, period of sleep is really a form of alcohol-induced coma. Not to be a party pooper, but in serious alcohol poisoning, it can lead to a terminal condition, which is why it's good to remember these simple facts that can show how much hooch you can handle and what effects it will have on you:

TABLE I

1-ounce Drinks per Hour	% of Alcohol in Blood	Results
1	.05 or less	Laid back, happy
2	0.7 to .1	Carefree, more outgoing, relaxed
3	.1 to .2	Speech and muscle control deteriorate
6	.2 to .4	Legless, incoherent, confused (in other words, truly newted)
More	.4 upwards	Comatose, suppression of autonomic functions like heart and lungs (definitely one foot in the grave, and can lead to two without medical attention)

The average body can absorb and handle about one ounce of 80-proof liquor in an hour. At this level it's possible to keep that rosy glow without getting wiped out—and even remain within the legal driving limits.

There's also another little secret, and that's your weight. During an average night's drinking, a 100-pound person will probably be juiced after four one-ounce drinks, while it would take some seven or eight of the same drinks to put a 240-pound hulk over the hill. I know, I've tried.

The legal definition of intoxication is accepted at about .1 percent of alcohol in the bloodstream.

Here's a simple reference table to show what the average social drinker can expect after guzzling specific amounts of booze. (See p. 127.)

And now we come to the biggie. Why do we get hangovers? The answer is not only what's really been going on in the head, but also what's been happening in another part of the body. The head counts, because those brain cells need to recover, but it's the liver that takes the biggest beating.

While all this booze is floating around your body, it's the liver's job to produce a number of chemical changes to filter the booze out and then send it on its way to the restroom. But if this process gets backed up by too much alcohol, the liver just simply can't handle those extra empties at the bar. Because alcohol is basically a poison, a lot of its toxic bad guys are escaping into the body instead of down the drain.

There's another reason for a hangover. Pure spirits like vodka do not have as many additives or impurities in them, but spirits like Scotch and bourbon, red wines, and beers do. These mean more strain on the liver because it has to work overtime to remove them, so if you want to be a purist drinker, and make it easier on the old breadbasket, it's best to stick to vodkas and white wines.

In a nutshell, the reason for a hangover is that the body hasn't been able to cope with getting rid of the booze as fast as it needs to, and while the wonderful effects on the brain have worn off, the body is still painfully trying to recover, without the benefit of that demon anesthetic.

Now that you know all that, let's get on with the fun.

PREVENTING A HANGOVER

Alcohol robs the body of essential vitamins. These are B_1, B_6, and C, and the lack of these vitamins can just add to the misery of a hangover. It also drains the minerals calcium, magnesium, and potassium. To cope with this, it's a good idea for a regular drinker to keep stocked up on vitamin and mineral supplements.

Another thing that alcohol does is dehydrate the body—that's why you wake up with parrot breath and a raging thirst after bashing the bottle.

The real secret to preventing a hangover is to slow down the process of absorption, and this can be done by eating foods that are rich in protein, oils, and milk, before or while you are drinking.

For this purpose, I suggest you wallop down my own special creation, a Pallbearer, before a night out on the tiles. (I call it that because it ensures you're not the one who's in the grave the next morning.) It will line your stomach and help slow down the effects of the booze.

PALLBEARER

8 ounces milk
1 egg
4 ounces orange juice
1 1/2 ounces orange liqueur

Put the milk and egg in a blender at low speed. Add orange juice and orange liqueur. For a frothier drink, you can add crushed ice.

Then, for dinner, eat foods that are high in protein, like fish dishes that contain some oils, and dairy products like cream or milk.

Later that night, after all the festivities are over and you're about to hit the sack, take a vitamin B-complex capsule, a vitamin C tablet, and a mineral supplement containing calcium, magnesium, and potassium. Add two aspirins or aspirin-free substitute, and chase the whole lot down with a very large glass of water.

Next morning you have an excellent chance of waking up bright-eyed and full of bounce with none of those painful aftereffects or any post-booze depression.

CURES

Take my advice. There's only two real cures when you're pollaxed with a hangover, either Band-Aids or more booze. You can gently patch up, or set back on the road to freedom with a carefully prescribed hair of the dog.

But watch those dog hairs! Whoa, they can be strong. I've even had them lead to an instant return bout the same morning, so you've gotta know what you're doing.

The first type of hangover cure normally replenishes the body with nutrients it needs to make a speedy recovery. The hair of the dog does mostly the same except that it pumps a little flush of alcohol back into the bloodstream to give you an instant shot in the arm. It also takes the brain cells out of shock and allows them to recover more gradually—and less painfully.

I prefer the hair of the dog for hangovers, but I've also included some emergency first-aid remedies that don't contain alcohol.

BASIC HAIR OF THE DOG

1 quick slug any brand of spirits

BEEFUP

1 teaspoon Bovril or beef extract
Hot water
1 shot vodka
1 squeeze of lemon juice
1 dash of pepper

Dissolve Bovril in hot water. Add remaining ingredients and let cool. Serve in a mug.

BETWEEN THE SHEETS

1/2 ounce Cointreau
1/2 ounce Bacardi rum
1/2 ounce brandy
1 teaspoon lemon juice

Shake ingredients in a mixing glass with ice and strain into a cocktail glass.

BITTER BLOW

8 ounces warm club soda
Large splash of angostura bitters

Stir together gently and serve in a highball glass.

BLACK VELVET

Cold champagne or strong sparkling cider
Guinness (at room temperature)

Pour both ingredients together into chilled champagne glass.

BLOODY MARY MORNING-AFTER

2 ounces premium chilled vodka
2 ounces chilled tomato juice
1 dash each Tabasco and Worcestershire sauce
1 dash teriyaki sauce (optional)
Celery salt
Black pepper
1 celery rib

In a mixing glass, add all ingredients except celery rib and shake well. Pour into tall, chilled glass. Garnish with celery.

CLAMATO BOOSTER   *8 ounces clam juice*
                          8 ounces tomato juice
                          1 ounce vodka
                          Juice of 1 lemon
                          Salt
                          Pepper
                          Dash teriyaki sauce

Mix ingredients in a blender or shaker. Serve over ice in an old-fashioned glass.

DOCTOR'S DELIGHT   *2 Alka-Seltzers*
                           8 ounces ginger ale
                           2 multi-vitamin capsules

Dissolve Alka-Seltzers in glass of ginger ale and use to chase down vitamins.

EGGNOG   *1 egg, separated*
                           4 tablespoons heavy cream
                           1 shot rum
                           Nutmeg

Mix yolk, cream, and rum. Let stand 1 hour. Beat egg white until stiff, then fold in and sprinkle with nutmeg. Serve in a cocktail glass.

FERNET BRANCA   *2 ounces drunk straight*

This is a black-liquid commerical preparation which is very popular in Britain and Europe. It can be found in good bars and liquor stores. It's made of a potent concoction of aromatic bitters and it runs at about 80 proof. Serve in shot glass.

It can also be diluted with sodas and drunk as a long, cool eye-opener.

HUNT'S BUNT

1/2 ounce chilled Russian vodka
1/2 ounce Myers's dark rum
1 1/2 ounces Baileys Irish cream
*   liqueur*

Mix vodka and rum with ice in a cocktail glass. Pour Irish cream over mixture. Sip through Irish cream.

IRISH WAKE-UP

3 ounces Irish whiskey
1 teaspoon sugar
4 whole cloves
2 tablespoons heavy cream
1 teaspoon
1 cup steaming, fresh coffee
Grated nutmeg

Fill tall, heatproof glass with coffee. Add Irish whiskey, sugar, and cloves, and place teaspoon in glass. When teaspoon has heated to same temperature as contents, hold it just under surface and slowly pour cream into teaspoon in glass (this should float the cream without mixing it). Sprinkle nutmeg on top.

LOU'S THREE C

1 1/2 ounces crème de cacao
2 ounces heavy cream
1 dash cinnamon

Add Crushed ice to cocktail glass. Stir in crème de cacao, heavy cream, garnish with cinnamon.

MOTHER'S MILK

12 ounces milk
1 tablespoon honey or molasses
1 dash vanilla, coffee, or chocolate
flavoring
1 pinch cinnamon

Gently heat the milk and honey. Add flavoring and cinnamon. When blended, sip in a warm mug.

PRAIRIE OYSTER

1 egg yolk
Celery salt
Freshly ground black pepper
1 tablespoon Worcestershire sauce
1 1/2 ounces port

Slip the egg yolk into glass without breaking it. Add salt, pepper, and sauce. Pour over port and swallow in one gulp. Serve in an old-fashioned glass.

SHANDY

Beer
Ginger ale

Best made with draught beer. Mix equal parts in a tall glass.

SHERRY-AID

2 ounces medium dry sherry
1 teaspoon confectioners' sugar
1 egg
Nutmeg to taste

Mix all ingredients in blender with plenty of ice. Pour into highball glass.

SINGAPORE SLING

*1/2 ounce Cherry Heering, or cherry
liqueur
1/2 ounce lemon juice
3 ounces gin*

Fill a cocktail glass with ice. Add ingredients. Top with water.

STALIN'S REVENGE

*2 ounces chilled Russian vodka
3 ounces cold clam juice
1 green olive*

Mix ingredients and serve in large martini glass or cocktail glass. Garnish with green olive.

SUFFERING BASTARD

*1 1/2 ounces brandy
1 1/2 ounces gin
1/2 ounce Rose's lime juice
2 dashes angostura bitters
Ginger ale splash*

Pour all ingredients except ginger ale into tall glass with ice. Add ginger ale.

SUPER BULLSHOT

*5 ounces cold consommé or beef
broth
1 dash horseradish
2 teaspoons Worcestershire sauce
Juice of 1 lemon
1 dash pepper
1 egg yolk*

Mix ingredients well. All in one gulp does the trick. Serve in a highball glass.

TAIL OF THE DOG   *2 ounces Scotch or bourbon*
1 tablespoon honey or syrup
`1 tablespoon heavy cream (not
whipped)

Blend ingredients with ice and strain to serve. This can also be made in a blender with ice cubes for a frosty crushed-ice drink. Serve in a highball glass.

UNDERBERG   *1 bottle taken neat*

Another popular, preprepared hair of the dog. It comes ready to knock back in a small, 2/3-ounce bottle. It's made of bitters and herbs and is 84 proof. It has a sweet taste of licorice. This can also be cut with sodas. Serve in a beer mug.

WHITE SHOULDERS   *1 1/2 ounces vodka*
1/2 ounce curaçao
1 ounce heavy cream

Put ingredients in a shaker with ice. Blend well and strain into a cocktail glass.

5

NORM ON BEER

A man without a beer is like a doctor without a condominium, a lawyer without a tongue, the Yankees with a manager, my wife without a complaint. . . .

A serious beer drinker treats his foamy brew with respect and pride. To the man who adores beer, the process that brought the golden goddess of drinks to him is the highest of art forms.

The fanatical beer drinker, like myself, is a man who puts his brew only second to God and Country. He is a stickler for detail; he knows exactly how much head should be on the glass, at precisely what angle a beer should be poured to create it, and at what temperature it should be presented to get both maximum taste and flavor.

The common beer drinker throws a six-pack into the back of his auto and expects it to perform to perfection; a beer expert has a cooler built in next to the car's air-conditioning outlet, always stores his brews upright, and never drinks directly from the bottle or can.

Let's get down to the serious business of beer, its history, the different types available, and some of the finer points of consuming this famous foam.

Beer is made by first malting barley, making it sprout by heat. This process helps break down the starch in the corn so that it will convert to sugar. Then the malt is mixed with hot water and the liquid, known as "wort," is drawn off and the residue discarded. Next a good helping of hops is added and the whole thing is boiled in a big vat. After it has cooled, the brew is drawn through ice-cold pipes into another vat and the yeast is added. Here it stays while the yeast does its job and turns the sugar into alcohol. After about six weeks we have BEER, ready to quaff.

Beer, I'll have you know, contains roughly 90 percent water, 3.6 percent alcohol, and the rest is carbonation. It is, pint for pint of alcohol content, the most expensive alcoholic drink in the world.

Another thing to remember when the five-o'clock-double-martini crowd shows up is that beer, with its low alcohol content, and high water content, is one of the least fattening drinks around.

There are six main types of beer, and all are distinctly different.

Lager is what we usually call beer in the United States. It is the youngest of the beers first made in Germany around 1840. *Lager,* literally translated, means "storage," and it revolutionized beers because of its long shelf life. It also turned the beer-making process upside down by starting the yeast fermentation process at the bottom of the vat instead of the top. Although it took three times as long for the yeast to work its way upwards to the top, it created a lighter, more delicate but more stable, brew which had extra gusto in its carbonation—more zip in its fizz, so to speak.

Ale isn't a true beer in the sense of the word at all. That's because it doesn't contain hops, the major ingredient for all beer flavor. Its chief ingredients are barley and malt, which make it a light, thirst-quenching brew. It is mainly an old English drink, but it's now becoming a popular import here in the good old U.S. of A.

Porter is another English invention that is darker, sweeter, and heavier than lager.

Bock is more European, mainly German, with a sweetish taste.

Pilsner is a distinctive beer that has its origins in the Czechoslovakian town of Pilsen. It is a light lager produced in a cooler-than-normal brewing process.

India ale was created purely out of necessity. During the great sailship days of the British Empire the British discovered, to their horror, that traditional ale didn't travel well and spoiled quickly during long voyages to far-off places like the Indies. So the English brewmasters solved the problem by creating India ale (also known as India pale ale). It has a higher alcohol content, is a heavier ale, and has more staying power.

Stout is the big daddy of them all and the only beer that is aged like a good wine. The Irish will tell you that a man is not a beer drinker unless he is a devotee of stout. The best-known stout worldwide is Guinness, the richest, darkest, heaviest, strongest, and creamiest of all the stouts. Stouts have up to 6 percent alcohol content and are almost jet black in color. What makes the difference is that a portion of the barley and malt is roasted, and a mega-dose of hops is added, to give it that distinct, robust flavor. With Guinness, it is stored in giant oak casks for a whole year until it is considered at the peak of perfection.

My buddy Cliff has come up with a mess of interesting tidbits about my favorite brew. Beer has a long history, but the first written record of a genuine brewery turned up on some baked clay tablets that date back to 6000 B.C. Those Egyptian brewmasters called it "hekit," a beverage made from barley and water and fermented by using bits of bread.

Brewing has always been a very serious business. For example, the Babylonians would not allow their brewmasters to have sexual contact with their wives and mistresses during the time that they had brews in the fermentation stage. (My wife came up with a similar suggestion the last time I came home stewed!)

The Children of Israel drank beer for purely medicinal purposes. They claimed it saved them from the plague, but the truth is that any drink with alcohol, and the power to kill germs, would probably have done the same.

For centuries, brewing beer was traditionally a woman's job around the home. In the medieval ages a woman was taken as a wife more for her brewing expertise than for what she could do in the kitchen or bedroom. (Ha!) Another little known fact is that Martha Washington, the little woman behind George, was an expert brewmaster, and she supervised all the beer making on their Virginia estate.

But it was religion that turned brewing into a fine art—or to be more accurate, the monks did. They brought science to brewing, and they were able to perfect the classic brews.

The idea was simple: give the people a better beer, say it's from God, and pack more parishoners into church, creating a good cash flow for building more monasteries. Monks, in effect, introduced the first beer monopolies. Once the monks had shown that beer making could be taken out of the home and turned into a big-bucks commercial concern, there followed a brewery-building explosion.

The brewery boom hit a peak in the United States just before prohibition in the twenties with some 1,500 breweries pumping out millions of gallons of suds a day—but since then, it's been downhill for independent brewers. After prohibition in 1933, only 800 independents opened their doors; by 1952, only 350 breweries had survived. In 1975, independent brewing was down to a mere dribble of only 70 concerns.

To the beer purist, it's very unfortunate because industry predictions show that by 1990 there may be only four giant breweries serving the whole United States—which narrows the taste-treat selection considerably.

But the shrinking breweries phenomenon is not just an American trend. In Great Britain there were some 2,900 family-owned breweries fifty years ago; now there are less than 100.

The bright side to all this—there is *always* a bright side to beer—is that with the consolidation of all these breweries, together with new scientific processes of brewing, today we are producing the finest beers the world has ever known.

With the introduction of the beer can, first test-marketed by the Gottfried Brewing Company of New Jersey as Krueger Cream Ale in 1935, we also found a lighter and less expensive way to distribute the brew—although some traditionalists still prefer the good old-fashioned glass bottle.

No matter how we drink it, or what brand it is, we in America love beer. We hoist our beer glasses and say "Cheers" some 43 billion times a year

BEER FACTS AND TRIVIA

Here are some fascinating foamy facts, which have all been verified by the Guinness people as authentic examples of our love for the brew:

The largest producing brewery in the world is the Anheuser-Busch brewery in St. Louis. In 1980, it set the world record for the greatest annual volume of beer ever produced by selling 50,200,000 barrels.

The largest brewery on a single site is the Adolph Coors brewery in Golden, Colorado, which produced 13,800,000 barrels in 1980.

The oldest brewery in the world is the Weihenstephan Brewery in Munich, West Germany, which was founded in A.D. 1040.

The largest exporter of ale and stout in the world is the giant Arthur Guinness and Sons brewery in Dublin, Ireland. It was founded in 1759 and ships out some 1.5 million glasses of brew every day.

The strongest beer ever produced was Samichlaus Bier, brewed in Germany by the Brauerai Hürlimann brewery. It cost about ten dollars a pint but had an alcohol content of 13.94 percent.

The weakest beer ever produced was also German. It was a sweet beer brewed by the Sunner Colne-Kalk Company in 1918 and contained less than .2 percent alcohol.

If I'd lived in Portland, Oregon, in the early 1900s, my favorite neighborhood watering hole would no doubt have been Erickson's. It had a bar that ran continuously around and across the main saloon, covering a staggering 684 feet.

The modern-day record for the longest bar is held by the

Working Men's Club in Mildura, Victoria, Australia, which has a 298-foot counter with twenty-seven beer pumps.

And if you are ever in Munich, West Germany, they'll no doubt find room for you at the Mathäser bar, where they can seat 5,500 people and serve an average of 100,800 pints of beer a day.

The largest collection of beer cans is owned by John F. Ahrens of Mount Laurel, New Jersey, who has over 13,000 different cans. In 1981, he sold one of them, a Rosalie Pilsner can, for $6,000.

If you ever need a coaster, try Leo Pisker of Vienna, who has the largest collection in the world, with 80,000 beer mats and coasters from 146 countries.

I thought I was a big beer drinker, but the real credit must go to my barroom buddie Steve Petrosino, who downed one liter of beer in 1.3 seconds in 1977 at the Gingerbreadman in Carlise, Pennsylvania. Or there's the famous Peter Dowdeswell of Northamptonshire, England, who drank two liters in 6 seconds in 1975, and also holds the world speed-drinking record for putting down two imperial pints of beer in 2.3 seconds, also in 1975. Pour me another, Coach.

MY HANDY TIPS FOR GETTING THE BEST OUT OF YOUR BEER

Beers need as much care and attention as their good neighbors on the bar, the wines and cognacs. Follow these handy hints and you shouldn't go wrong:

• Ideally, beer should be served at a temperature of 42 degrees and ale at 55 degrees. Most imported beers should be 48 to 50 degrees, with the exceptions of Guinness and Bass ale, which should be chilled to 55 degrees. Needless to say, beer tastes better the nearer it is to its ideal temperature.

• Glasses are great for beer, but the serious slow sipper will prefer a stein with a hinged lid to keep the beer fresher longer.

• Never wash beer glasses or mugs in soap and water. They should be cleansed only in a solution of soda or salt and left to dry naturally. This is one of the secrets to keeping a great head on beer.

• Beer that is too cold will appear cloudy and have a weak head. You can't see this with canned beers, so watch how much you cool them.

• Do not shake, jiggle, or bounce around bottles or cans of beer. Who wants to lose half of it when you open them, anyway?

• Sunlight can spoil the perfection of bottled beer. It's better to hide beer away in the shade or store in a cellar.

• Never store beer in the freezer, the coolest compartment of your refrigerator, or up against ice.

• When mixing stouts with lighter beers or ginger ale, always pour the stout in last. This will avoid an exploding head and wasteful runover. Heaven forbid.

• To create a good head on beer, always hold the bottle or glass at a slant and run the beer down the side of the glass— inside the glass, of course.

• Never store beer in a warm place.

• When you are dealing with bottle caps and plunger can openers, always open briskly to avoid spraying.

• For those of you who don't have salt problems in your diet, a pinch of salt will liven up the head of most "dead" beers.

• Never try to serve "day-after" keg beers once they have been sitting in the sun without being iced down. They may have spoiled.

• Next time you're making a mixed drink, try using beer instead of soda. You'll be surprised how versatile beer can be. Here are two recipes in which you can substitute beer as a mixer.

BARIOS SUPER SUDS

2 ounces Tequila
1/2 ounce crème de cassis
1 1/2 teaspoons Rose's Lime Juice
Beer
1 slice lime

Fill a tall glass with ice. Add first 3 ingredients, and then fill to top of glass with beer. Garnish with lime slice.

TOM COLLINS BROTHER

1 1/2 ounces gin
2 teaspoons superfine sugar
1/2 ounce Rose's Lime Juice
Beer
1 slice lemon

Fill a Tom Collins glass with ice. Add first 3 ingredients, and then fill to top of glass with beer. Garnish with lemon slice.

• Avoid a beer that comes out of the bottle or can flat. It's either older than it should be, or the container may have punctured. Either way, it's unsanitary.
• For a real expert education in beer, try brewing your own. Simple starter kits are available from many stores, and they produce jugs of beer that only cost pennies—and a little bit of patience and time and effort.

Well, Coach, one more and then I'm outta here!

6

SAM'S NONALCOHOLIC DRINKS

One thing I've learned is that whether you're behind the bar fixing a few drinks for friends, or pitching hard in front of 50,000 fans, you gotta give the people what they want. There are a lot of ladies and gents out there who would like nothing better than a good nonalcoholic drink, and they are some of the hardest partiers I know. In fact, in my pitching days, lots of guys on the team would celebrate in the clubhouse after a big win with soft drinks. You just can't down the hard stuff and stay on top of your game the next day.

So the next time you're having some buddies over for a couple of tall ones, make sure to treat the teetotalers and cocktail drinkers with the same care. My nonalcoholic drink recipes do just that.

They're bound to please. They're easy to prepare, with juices, mixers, milk, ice cream, and chocolate as the main

Note: In all of the following recipes, except the two low-cal eggnogs, ice cream can be substituted for milk or yogurt, and vice versa.

ingredients. And they taste so good, they're guaranteed to make any guest feel special.

And at your next party, when a seductive little lady wanders by and says she'd sure like to stay, but doesn't drink alcohol . . . don't feel like you've just struck out—whip her up one of my specialties. It always works for me.

COCKTAILS AND TALL DRINKS

ANGOSTURA HIGHBALL

12 ounces ginger ale
2 dashes angostura bitters

Fill a highball glass with ice. Add ginger ale, stir, and add bitters. Serves 1.

APPLE SPARKLE

4 ounces club soda
4 ounces apple juice
1 lemon slice

Put 2 ice cubes in a cocktail glass. Add equal parts soda and apple juice. Garnish with lemon slice. Serves 1.

ARYAN

1 pint plain yogurt
16 ounces cold water
2 tablespoons crushed dried mint

Put yogurt and water into a blender. Blend at high speed until well mixed and smooth. Add dried mint and blend again. Chill thoroughly and serve in a tall glass filled with ice. Makes 4 4-ounce servings.

AVOCADO APERITIF

1 medium avocado
1 large cucumber
1 tablespoon olive oil
Juice of 1 lemon
1/2 cup chopped parsley
2 lemon slices, halved

Peel the avocado and cucumber, cut into sections, and place in blender. Add next 3 ingredients and blend until smooth. Strain into chilled glasses and garnish with lemon slices. Makes 4 4-ounce servings.

BANANA DAIQUIRI

1 large banana
3/4 cup crushed ice
8 ounces grapefruit juice

Blend all ingredients at high speed in blender until frothy. Makes 2 8-ounce or 4 4-ounce servings.

BLACK AND TAN

8 ounces chilled cola
4 ounces milk

Fill an 8-ounce glass with 3 ice cubes and add cola until the glass is 2/3 full. Add milk to fill and stir gently. Serves 1.

BOSTON TOMATO COCKTAIL

8 ounces tomato juice
1 1/2 tablespoons lime juice
8 ounces clam juice
1 dash Tabasco
Salt

Put all ingredients in a blender and blend at high speed for 1 minute. Serve in a chilled, 12-ounce highball glass. Serves 1.

CITRUS COCKTAIL

8 ounces grapefruit juice
4 ounces orange juice
1 tablespoon sugar
4 ounces undiluted evaporated milk

Mix juices with sugar. Pour into a 12-ounce glass filled with ice. Pour in evaporated milk, stirring constantly to prevent curdling. Serves 1.

CLAM JUICE COCKTAIL

8 ounces V-8 juice
8 ounces clam juice
1 teaspoon minced onion
1 dash Tabasco
Celery leaves

Put all ingredients in a blender and blend at high speed for at least 1 minute. Serve in a chilled 12-ounce cocktail glass. Garnish with celery leaves. Serves 1.

HOLIDAY COCKTAIL

16 ounces sweet cider
1/2 cup raw cranberries
1 medium banana
1/2 cup sunflower seeds
1 cup crushed ice

Put all ingredients in a blender and blend for at least 1 minute. Strain, if desired, into 3 chilled cocktail glasses. Serves 3.

ORANGE DAIQUIRI

8 ounces apple juice
1 teaspoon honey
1 cup crushed ice
1 dash cinnamon
1 banana

1 whole orange, peeled and cut into
 chunks
1 orange slice, or twist of orange
 peel

Put all ingredients except orange slice into a blender and blend until well mixed and frothy. Pour into a tall iced-tea or collins glass and garnish with orange slice or a twist of orange peel. Serves 1.

PIÑA COLADA

2 tablespoons coconut cream
6 ounces pineapple juice
1 teaspoon lime juice
1 teaspoon lemon juice
1 lemon slice
1 lime slice

Put first 4 ingredients into a blender. Blend until frothy. Pour into a glass half filled with crushed ice and garnish with fruit slices. Serves 1.

PINK LADY

8 ounces lemonade
1 cup fresh raspberries
1 scoop vanilla ice cream
1 sprig mint leaves

Put all ingredients except mint into a blender and blend until frothy and well mixed. Pour into a chilled 12-ounce glass. Garnish with a fresh raspberry and mint sprig. Serves 1.

PUSSYFOOT

3 ounces cup orange juice
3 ounces cup pineapple juice
1 teaspoon grenadine
4 ounces ginger ale
1 orange slice
1 lemon peel

Fill a collins glass with 3 ice cubes. Add juices and grenadine and mix until well blended. Add ginger ale to fill, stirring gently to blend. Garnish with slice of orange and twist lemon peel over drink and add to glass. Serves 1.

RUSSIAN ICED TEA

1 quart water plus 1 cup
2 heaping tablespoons Darjeeling
 tea leaves
3 cups sugar
8 ounces lemon juice
1 cup fresh mint leaves
Lemon slices
Sprigs of mint

Bring 1 quart water to a boil. Pour it into a container over tea leaves and allow to sit 3 hours before straining. Make a syrup of sugar and 1 cup cold water by boiling mixture for 10 minutes. Remove from the heat, stir in lemon juice, and add mint leaves. At the end of the 3 hours strain both liquids into a large container and stir until well mixed. Serve in 12-ounce glasses filled with crushed ice and garnish with lemon slices and fresh mint sprigs. Makes 10 4-ounce servings.

SARATOGA

2 tablespoons lemon juice
1/2 teaspoon sugar
2 dashes angostura bitters
Ginger ale

Put 2 or 3 ice cubes in a tall glass. Add lemon juice, sugar, and bitters. Stir to blend well and add ginger ale to fill glass. Stir gently. Serves 1.

SCORPION

2 ounces orange juice
1/2 ounce pineapple juice
1 1/2 ounces lemon juice

1/2 ounce orgeat syrup
1/2 cup crushed ice
1 gardenia

Place all ingredients into blender. Blend well and pour into a tall glass. Float a gardenia on top as garnish and serve with a straw. Serves 1.

ST. PATRICK'S LIMELIGHT

12 ounces cups pineapple juice
1 teaspoon finely grated lime rind
2 ounces cup lime juice
1 medium ripe banana
3 green Maraschino cherries
Green food coloring
1 pint vanilla ice cream

Fill a blender with all ingredients and blend at high speed until smooth. Makes 4 8-ounce servings.

SUNSET

4 ounces cup orange juice
2 tablespoons grenadine, plus a
   dash
4 ounces cup pineapple juice
1 lemon slice

In a large, stem glass filled with ice cubes, add grenadine, pineapple, and orange juice. Garnish with lemon slice. Add a dash of grenadine to the top. Serves 1

TOMATO JUICE ITALIAN

8 ounces tomato juice
1 red onion slice
Salt and pepper to taste
4 fresh basil leaves
1 fresh oregano leaf

Pour all ingredients into a blender. Run at high speed until well mixed. Serve over ice in a tall, 12-ounce chilled glass. Serves 1.

VIRGIN CAESAR

4 ounces cup clam juice
2 drops Tabasco
Salt and pepper to taste
4 ounces cup V-8 juice
4 drops Worcestershire sauce

Put all ingredients into blender and blend until frothy. Add crushed ice. Blend ½ minute more and pour into a chilled collins glass containing 2 ice cubes. Serves 2.

VIRGIN MARY

8 ounces tomato juice
2 drops Tabasco
Salt and pepper to taste
4 drops Worcestershire sauce
1 celery rib

Put all ingredients except celery in a blender and blend until frothy. Pour over ice in a tall 12-ounce glass. Garnish with celery and serve with a short straw. Serves 1.

COFFEE AND HOT DRINKS

CAFÉ AU LAIT

Sugar (optional)
8 ounces strong, hot coffee
8 ounces hot milk

Prepare 2 coffee mugs. If sugar is used place the desired amount in the bottom of the mugs. Pour the coffee and hot milk into the mugs simultaneously. Milk should not be allowed to boil. Serves 2.

CAFÉ BORGIA

8 ounces hot Italian coffee
8 ounces hot chocolate
Sweetened heavy cream
1 orange peel, grated

While coffee and chocolate are heating, whip the sweetened heavy cream. Pour equal quantities of hot coffee and hot chocolate into 2 warmed mugs. Top with whipped cream and sprinkle with the orange peel as a garnish. Serves 2.

COFFEE CAPPUCCINO

8 ounces hot milk
2 teaspoons sugar
8 ounces hot Italian espresso
Cinnamon

Heat milk, but do not allow it to boil. Put sugar in bottom of 2 warmed mugs. Pour equal amounts hot coffee and milk into cups at the same time. Sprinkle with cinnamon. Serves 2.

COFFEE CHOCACCINO

8 ounces strong, hot coffee
1 ounce melted chocolate
1 tablespoon heavy cream, whipped
Cinnamon

Put a little hot coffee in the bottom of a warmed glass. Add chocolate and stir to mix well. Fill with remainder of the hot coffee. Add whipped cream and shake a little cinnamon on top. Serves 1.

CRANBERRY GLOGG

40 ounces cranapple juice
4 orange slices
1/2 teaspoon cinnamon
1/2 cup raisins
1/4 cup cranberries
8 whole cloves
1/2 teaspoon cardamom

Heat all ingredients in a medium saucepan. Do not allow to boil. Allow to cool overnight. Bring to boil the next day and simmer for 30 minutes. Serve warm in mugs. Serves 6.

HOT APPLE TODDY

8 ounces apple juice
1/2 teaspoon brown sugar
1 cinnamon stick
1 whole clove
1 lemon slice
1/4 teaspoon butter

Heat apple juice to a boil. Pour into mug and add brown sugar. Add cinnamon stick, clove, and butter. Stir until butter melts. Garnish with lemon slice. Serves 1.

HOT FRUIT DRINK

32 ounces orange juice
1/4 cup sugar
1 teaspoon whole cloves
3 cinnamon sticks
1 teaspoon grated lemon
4 orange slices

Put all ingredients except orange slices in a pan and gently heat to boiling. Reduce heat. Simmer for 5 minutes. Strain into 4 mugs. Garnish with orange slices. Makes 4 10-ounce servings.

MEXICAN CHOCOLATE

48 ounces milk
3/4 cup cinnamon
3/4 cup coarsely chopped sweet
   baking chocolate, plus some for
   garnish
6 tablespoons whipped heavy cream

Heat all ingredients except cream and beat constantly while heating. Serve with whipped cream and garnish with grated chocolate. Serves 6.

MOCA FROTH

8 ounces hot coffee
8 ounces hot cocoa
1/2 cup whipped heavy cream
Grated chocolate

Heat coffee and cocoa together. Do not allow mixture to boil. Pour into cups, top with whipped cream, and grate chocolate over the top. Serves 2.

SPICED LEMONADE

8 ounces sugar syrup (Karo)
12 whole cloves
1 cinnamon stick
12 ounces lemon juice
32 ounces water

Put sugar syrup, cloves, and cinnamon in a small saucepan and heat on a low flame for 5 minutes. Add lemon juice and let stand for 1 hour. Strain and combine with the water in a pitcher. Serve it tumblers filled with crushed ice. Makes 12 4-ounce servings.

VIENNESE COFFEE

4 ounces heavy cream
1 tablespoon confectioners' sugar
24 ounces hot, very strong coffee
1/2 teaspoon vanilla extract

Combine heavy cream, sugar, and vanilla. Beat until stiff. Pour coffee into 4 cups. Float whipped cream mixture on top. Serves 4.

WHITE LIGHTNING

24 ounces white grape juice
8 ounces grapefruit juice
32 ounces cranberry juice
1 lemon, sliced

Put all the juices and lemon in a large saucepan and bring to a boil. Cover and simmer 10 minutes. Remove lemon slices. Serve hot in mugs. Makes 16 4-ounce servings.

EGGNOGS

BANANA NOG

24 ounces chilled milk
4 ice cubes
2 eggs
1 cup mashed bananas
1 tablespoon honey
8 ounces club soda
Lime and banana slices

Put first 5 ingredients into a blender and blend well. Add club soda and stir a couple of times. Pour into large, chilled glasses and garnish with lime and banana slices. Makes 4 8-ounce servings.

EGGNOG

1 egg
1 tablespoon superfine sugar
^{1}/4 teaspoon vanilla
Dust of nutmeg
8 ounces milk

Put all ingredients except nutmeg into a blender and blend until frothy. Pour into highball glass and garnish with nutmeg. Serves 1.

GENERAL HARRISON'S EGGNOG TREAT

1 egg
^{1}/2 cup crushed ice
1 teaspoon superfine sugar
8 ounces sweet cider
Dust of nutmeg

Combine egg, ice, and sugar in cocktail shaker and shake until frothy and well mixed. Strain into a 12-ounce collins glass. Fill to the top with cider and stir gently. Dust with nutmeg. Serves 1.

LIME EGGNOG
(Low-Cal)

Any low-cal liquid sweetener
3 tablespoons lime juice
2 small eggs, separated
Salt
20 ounces skim milk

Add liquid sweetener to lime juice. Beat egg yolks and add salt. Mix into lime juice and blend until fluffy. Stir in milk and chill. Beat egg whites until they form stiff peaks and fold half of mixure into lime juice. Use other half to garnish punch. Makes 2 12-ounce servings.

ORANGE EGGNOG

3 tablespoons frozen orange juice
8 ounces chilled milk
1 egg

Put all ingredients into a blender and blend until frothy. Strain into a chilled 12-ounce glass. Serves 1.

VITA EGGNOG
(Low-Cal)

4 ounces skim milk
1 egg
8 ounces apple juice

Blend all ingredients in a blender on high speed for 10 seconds. Pour into glasses. Makes 2 6-ounce servings.

PUNCHES

ANGEL PUNCH

1 cup sugar syrup
16 ounces lemon juice
32 ounces strong green tea
64 ounces white grape juice
2 28-ounce bottles club soda

Mix all ingredients except club soda and put into the refrigerator until well chilled. Put a block of ice in a punch bowl and pour chilled mixture over it. Add club soda and stir gently. Makes 42 4-ounce servings.

BIG PARTY PUNCH

3 cups sugar
96 ounces pineapple juice
8 ounces lime juice
24 ounces orange juice
12 ounces lemon juice
1/2 cup fresh mint leaves
2 28-ounce bottles ginger ale
28-ounce bottle club soda
2 cups halved strawberries
Orange and lemon slices

Mix sugar and juices into blender. Chill for a couple of hours with mint leaves. Strain over a block of ice into a punch bowl. Pour ginger ale and club soda into bowl, stirring slightly to combine ingredients. Add strawberries and fruit slices. Makes 70 4-ounce servings.

BRUNCH PUNCH

*16-ounce can frozen grapefruit
    concentrate
6-ounce can frozen orange
    concentrate
6-ounce can frozen lemon
    concentrate
64-ounce bottle cranberry cocktail
2 28-ounce bottles club soda
2 28-ounce bottles ginger ale
Orange and lemon slices
Lime slices*

Let frozen juice concentrates defrost and then mix together well. Pour over a large block of ice in a punch bowl. Add cranberry juice and stir well, until mixture is well blended and chilled. Add soda and ginger ale around the edges and stir slightly to mix. Add fruit slices for garnish. Makes 50 4-ounce servings.

**CARRY NATION
PUNCH**

*8 ounces sugar syrup
32 ounces orange juice
24 ounces lemon juice
8 ounces pineapple juice
2 28-ounce bottles ginger ale
Lemon slices
Orange slices*

Blend sugar syrup and juices to mix well. Pour over a block of ice in a punch bowl. Add ginger ale around the edges and stir gently. Garnish with fruit slices. Makes 35 4-ounce servings.

EASY PUNCH

*16-ounce can lemonade concentrate
1 package frozen strawberries
1 medium can crushed pineapple,
    12-15 ounces
3 28-ounce bottles ginger ale*

Place lemonade concentrate and fruit into a blender. Blend until well mixed. Put fruit mixture in a punch bowl containing ice cubes. Add ginger ale. Makes 30 3-ounce servings.

FLORIDA CRUSH

6-ounce can frozen orange juice
  concentrate
15 ounces cold water
4 lime slices
4 mint sprigs

Fill glasses half full with crushed ice. Add orange juice concentrate and water and stir to blend. Garnish each glass with a slice of lime and a mint sprig. Makes 4 6-ounce servings.

FLORIDA PUNCH

2 cups superfine sugar
128 ounces orange-grapefruit juice
12 ounces lime juice
20 ounces cold water
48 ounces ginger ale
Orange and lime slices

Stir sugar into juices until dissolved. (This may be heated slightly to make the job easier.) Chill for at least 2 hours. Add cold water and stir. Fill 8-ounce goblets with ice cubes. Combine sweetened fruit juices and ginger ale in a chilled punch bowl (ice ring optional). Stir to blend well and garnish with fruit slices. Makes 26 8-ounce servings.

GRAPEFRUIT BANANA DAIQUIRI PUNCH

12 1/2-ounce can frozen grapefruit
  juice
3 large ripe bananas
32 ounces cold water
Mint leaves

Put juice and bananas into a blender. Add water. Blend until smooth. Pour into a punch bowl containing ice cubes and garnish with mint leaves. Makes 6 8-ounce servings.

HOT GRAPE PUNCH

32 ounces bottled grape juice
1 teaspoon cinnamon
1/8 teaspoon ginger
1/2 cup sugar
1/4 teaspoon nutmeg
1 dash ground cloves
4 cinnamon sticks

Combine all ingredients except cinnamon sticks in a stainless steel or enamel pot. Bring to a boil slowly. Serve in hot mugs with cinnamon stick for stirring. Makes 4 8-ounce servings.

PENSACOLA PUNCH

2 cups superfine sugar
48 ounces water
46 ounces grapefruit juice
28 ounces lime juice
1 pound grapefruit sections
Lime slices
Maraschino cherries
Mint leaves

Stir sugar, water, and juices together in a saucepan over a low heat until all the sugar is dissolved. Cool. Chill for at least 2 hours and then pour over crushed ice in a punch bowl. Add grapefruit sections and garnish with lime slices, cherries, and mint leaves. Makes 32 4-ounce servings.

SUNNY SANGRIA

4 ounces orange juice
32 ounces grape juice
4 ounces lemon juice
32 ounces club soda
1 orange, sliced thin
1 lemon, sliced thin

Mix fruit juices together in a blender. Fill glasses with ice cubes. Pour in juice mixture until glasses are half filled. Fill to top with club soda. Garnish with fruit slices. Makes 18 4-ounce servings.

SPICED CIDER CUP *32 ounces sweet cider*
1 cinnamon stick
1/4 teaspoon whole allspice
1/4 cup sugar
1/2 teaspoon whole cloves
4 half lemon slices

Combine all ingredients in a saucepan and heat to boiling point. Remove from heat and allow mixture to sit for 4 or 5 hours. Strain, chill, and serve in tall glasses filled with ice. Drink may be reheated and served in mugs. Makes 4 8-ounce servings.

SPICED PARTY PUNCH *12 whole cloves*
4 cinnamon sticks
72 ounces pineapple juice
36 ounces water
2 48-ounce bottles cranberry juice

Place cloves and cinnamon sticks in a percolator basket. Put the remaining ingredients in the coffeepot. Bring to a boil and perk for 10 minutes. Serve hot. Makes 50 4-ounce servings.

TEA PUNCH *24 ounces strong black tea*
32 ounces orange juice
16 ounces raspberry syrup
1 cup crushed pineapple
8 ounces lime juice
64 ounces chilled club soda
Orange slices

Pour all ingredients except soda over ice in a punch bowl, adding soda just before serving. Garnish with orange slices. Makes 40 4-ounce servings.

7

CLIFF ON TOASTS

Folks have been raising goblets and glasses to each other for centuries, but the first real "toast" actually happened in a way like this:

In the distant mists of time in a dark medieval castle, a king gave out a large goblet of mead to be passed around to his assembled noblemen.

The king exclaimed, "Drink healthy my men . . . and the last one down gets to eat that piece of moldy toast in the bottom!"

Nobody has ever been quite clear why the piece of toast was in the goblet in the first place; it might have been just an accident, or a little joke by the king. But from that moment on, it became very chic at baronial banquets and ancient weekend cookouts to float a piece of toast, or a crouton, in the drink. Historians of drinking practices have explained that the toast came to be taken as a sign of food or sustenance to go with the drink.

What really matters is that the word *toast* stuck and became synonymous with the traditional practice of saying a few words before raising a glass to drink to your fellow man. Today toasts are used for every occasion in which drink is involved and words need to be said. They can be sentimental, comic, lyrical, long and laborious, short and sweet, or even one-worders.

The most typical one-word toasts are: in France, *"Santé!"*; in Germany, *"Prosit!"*; in Spanish-speaking countries, *"Salud!"*; in Scandanavia, *"Skoal!"*; in Italy, *"Salute!"*; and in English, our very own *"Cheers!"*

The original act of raising glasses and clinking them together is even older than the spoken toast and may have had mystical or religious significance. It seems that during the early Christian era, the sound of clinking glasses sounded very much like a bell—and the ringing of bells was known to repell the devil.

Toasting has not been without its bizarre practices, though. The Vikings, who you'll remember were extravagant partygoers and plunderers, found that after all the pillaging and raping was over, the next best thing to Valhalla was to drink your ale and mead from the skulls of your fallen enemies. Yum. A little known fact is that the name for these cranium cups became *skoal* in Norse, and *skiel* in Scottish and Celtic, both meaning "bowl," and led to our present toast, "Skoal!"

The French, never far behind the fashions, also got into the act. A certain French tribe, called the Guebres, liked to dig up the heads of their forefathers and use the skulls as drinking vessels. This may have originated the word "skulduggery."

But toasts really caught on in Britain during the mid-seventeenth century when the floating of croutons in the drink began to take on a more scientific value. It was probably around 1650 that spiced or flavored toast was added to the drinks to enhance the taste. More accurately, it was added to mask some of the foul tastes of poorly produced wines of that time. Whichever way you look at it, using these flavorings produced the forerunners of our flavored liqueurs, like cherry brandy and anisette.

Another theory is that, since toasts are almost always made toward the end of a ceremony's festivities, the toasted bread in the glass may have acted like a sponge to absorb the residue and sediment from the bottom of the wine or mead barrel.

The English settlers carried their toasts, together with their flagons of wine and ale, to the New World. Americans, being gregarious folk, fell in love with the idea, and toasts were here to stay. We refined them into a new art form that fit in with a very traditional American theory: if it's bigger, it's better.

Take the example of a certain Captain McDougal and his forty-four friends, who held a cozy little dinner together back in 1744 in New York City. The record shows that Captain McDougal et al. drank forty-five toasts during the dinner using fifteen different kinds of wine and two types of beer. (They also consumed forty-five pounds of steak.)

Toasts usually were popular catchphrases of the day. While some have kept their original meanings, most of the original sentiments have fallen by the barstool. A good example is "Here's mud in your eye!" Ask ten people what it means or where it came from and you'll be lucky if anyone knows the right answer. In fact, there are a number of right answers because, like many toasts, they tend to borrow from earlier phrases and adapt them to modern situations.

An early Irish version of "mud in your eye" is plainly understood when quoted in full. The exact toast reads, "Here's mud in your eye while I look over your lovely sweetheart!"

And when the early settlers arrived in America and began to move West, "mud in your eye" took on a whole new meaning. When a prospective pioneer was about to go West, he would visit his local tavern, in Boston or New York, where his friends would toast "mud in your eye." It was a toast to the hope that the farmer would find rich, fertile—and moist—soil that would splash up into his face as he plowed his furrows.

Toasts have been written by just about every literary great who has set pen to paper, and it's become a tradition for a man of the written word to produce at least one immortal toast in his lifetime. Writers do tend to find a lot of their inspiration in bars, so it's only natural that they should honor the source of at least some of their genius.

Among the notables who have written famous toasts are William Shakespeare (in just about every one of his plays), Charles Dickens, Ralph Waldo Emerson, Herman Melville, Oliver Wendell Holmes, Mark Twain, and even Charles VI.

But not all toasts are written by the greats. Many of the most memorable come from Irish and European folklore, and Yiddish history; their authors long since passed into antiquity and anonymity.

Some toasts are much more recent, but no less memorable. Remember the scene in the movie *Casablanca* when Humphrey Bogart, as Rick, raises his glass to Ingrid Bergman and says the immortal words "Here's lookin' at you, kid!"? Boy, who could forget?

Others are less memorable, like the one from the literary light who wrote a toast to "hay fever," which ended with the wonderfully forgettable line, "Here's looking at-choo!" (Coach told me that one!)

Toasts weren't always popular, either. Another little known fact is that during the Middle Ages, the Church of England had a sudden ban on toasts made to salute the dead. It was considered "barbaric" and "unholy" to drink to the well-being of "absent friends."

And in the American Colonies, the Commonwealth of Massachusetts effected a law that made drinking to another person's health illegal. It was considered a "useless ceremony" and an "abominable practice." The law was repealed twelve years later, in 1645.

The credit for one of the most generous toasts of all has to go to Douglas McElvy of New York, who, after his death in 1973, left $12,000 in his will for his barroom cronies to toast him on the anniversary of his death. They must have been big drinkers because the toast fund only lasted three years. But today the tradition still lives on, though the money is gone, and those same cronies chip in each New Year's Day to drink "memorial" gin and tonics and toast McElvy's empty barstool.

How did our own "Cheers" find its way into toast-drinking history? It most likely came from a nineteenth-century toast to Queen Victoria. The full toast to Her Majesty was "Nine times nine cheers!", which was eventually shortened to simply "Cheers!"

As well as toasting your favorite friends with "Cheers," here are samples of well-known toasts that should supply a suitable sentiment for just about every occasion.

TOASTS FOR EVERY OCCASION

Eat, drink, and be merry,
For tomorrow you may diet!

Here's to my friend. He knows me well
And likes me just the same.

Here's to our wives and sweethearts:
May they never meet!

To the men I've loved
To the men I've kissed
To heartfelt apologies
To the men I've missed.

Say it with jewelry,
Say it with drink,
But always be careful
Never to say it with ink!

Drink and the world drinks with you;
Stop, and you sit alone!

A toast to the Three Great American Birds:
May you always have
An Eagle in your pocket,
A Turkey on the table,
And an Old Crow in your glass.

Here's to the friend who's never blue,
Here's to the buddy ever true,
Here's to the pal, no matter what the load,
Who never turns down my one for the road.

A glass in the hand is worth two on the shelf,
So drink it down and enjoy yourself.

One drink is plenty;
Two drinks too many,
And three not half enough!

One swallow does not a summer make,
But it sure breaks a New Year's resolution!

To the cocktail party where olives are speared—
And friends stabbed!

Here's to friendship . . . a deeper emotion
than love,
But not half as entertaining.

Here's to my home sweet home,
There's no place like it, after the bars close.

Here's a toast to time,
Boy, how it flies when you're getting bombed.

*Here's to the morning after and the
good times I must have had.*

*I used to know a clean toast, but now I
cannot think of it.
So fill your glass with anything, and bless
our souls we'll drink to it.*

10. You can create a contest and make some money with these word games. Get everybody around the bar to chip in a dollar in a pool, and the first person to get the most right answers wins. Of course, you will win because you've already studied the words, that is unless they've read the book as well.

a) See how many words you can come up with that begin and end with the same two letters. Here are some words to start off with:

> periscope
> iconoclastic
> enliven
> amalgam

b) For this, you already have to have set up a buddy who will supply the most impossible words in the dictionary for the group to spell. The odds of getting ten in a row correct are 10,000 to 1. (Of course, you will have already seen the words beforehand and committed them to memory.) Here are some suggestions:

bureaucracy	opalescence	acquiesce	entrepreneur
debauchery	poseur	pterodactyl	cellist
eschew	veterinary	catarrh	tabernacle
separate	quorum	iridescent	diuresis
impugn	queue	connoisseur	barbiturate

11. Write these words down on a sheet of paper and bet your friends they won't see what they have in common.

definition	sleighing
stupid	nope
hijack	sturgeon
coughing	first

Answer: They each contain consecutive letters of the alphabet.

12. Here's another water trick. Bet some patsy five dollars that you can move the water from a saucer to a brandy snifter without touching the saucer. Then ask the bartender to pour some water into a saucer and lend you a brandy snifter. Take a book of matches from the bar, light one, and hold it under the glass for a few seconds. Then place the glass upside down over the saucer and, amazingly enough, the vacuum from the heat will draw the water up into the glass.

13. Scramble the names of some of our favorite football or baseball players on a piece of paper and bet your buddies they can't figure them out in three minutes or less. Always give yourself a fighting chance and make sure they've had a couple of drinks beforehand.

Example: GOGSB (BOGGS)
           SNVAE (EVANS)
           NELOLNSA (ALLENSON)
           KRAJU (JURAK)
           FDLIWEIN (WINFIELD)
           LOYRAB (BAYLOR)

14. Bet a disbeliever that you can pick up three matches with a fourth one, all at the same time. Wait until he puts his money up on the bar and then take three matches and arrange them in a tripod like an Indian teepee and set them on fire. Blow the flames out just as the heads begin to fuse together and you will be able to lift all three with the fourth match.

15. Here's a wager you should try on a math major. Bet a free beer that you can take one from twenty-nine and still end up with thirty.
Answer: You do it in numerals. XXIX stands for twenty-nine. Take away I and you have XXX, which equals thirty.

JOKES

1. A fellow came into a bar and started complaining to the bartender. "I've got a problem with my dog and I don't know what to do about it."

"What's wrong?" asked the bartender.

"He's got ticks."

Said the bartender, "Why don't you wind him?"

2. A man is sitting at the bar when a Salvation Army worker comes in and taps him on the shoulder. "Excuse me, brother, do you love your neighbor?" he asks.

"Oh, I tried to," said the man, "but she won't let me."

3. Two tourists sitting in a bar were amazed at the speed in which a local drinker could pack away the beer. So they bet him twenty dollars that he couldn't drink ten pints in twenty minutes. The drunk asked for a few minutes to get ready and he went out of the door of the pub and came back twenty minutes later. The tourists ordered the pints set up in front of him and he drank them down in record time. "I knew I could do it," he said when being congratulated. "I just did it in the pub down the road."

4. Two old men were sitting at a bar which had been newly remodeled and had a spanking new jukebox in the corner.

"You know," said one to the other, "I miss the old days and the old ways. I especially miss the old spittoon that used to be in the corner."

"You always did," said the friend.

5. A drunk was brought before the judge for disturbing the peace. Said the judge, "You know, it's alcohol and alcohol alone that is responsible for your condition."

"Well, thank goodness for that," replied the drunk. "I thought it was my fault."

6. A man was sitting at the bar when another customer came over and took the stool next to him. "Excuse me," said the first man, "but I couldn't help noticing that you're wearing one red sock and one green one. Isn't that an unusual combination?"

"Yes, it is," replied the man. "And you know, I have another pair at home just like it."

7. A customer was explaining to the bartender how his drinking problem got started. "For months I didn't know where my wife was spending her evenings. Then one night I went home, and there she was."

8. The drunk saw the duck hunter lying in the rushes poised with his gun ready in the direction of the high-flying flock. "Shay, mishter," advised the drunk, "don't waisht a shot on them. The falls enough to kill 'em."

9. The drunk was brought into night court, having been picked up on suspicion of being the notorious night prowler. "What were you doing out at 3 A.M.?" the judge asked.

"I was going to a lecture."

"A lecture at 3 A.M.?" The judge said scornfully.

"Oh sure," said the drunk. "And shomestimesh my wife even shtays up longer than that."

10. A man walks into a bar with a stalk of celery behind his ear. And he does the same thing for thirty days after that. Finally he shows up with a carrot behind his ear and the bartender can't control his curiosity any longer. He asks the man why he's wearing the carrot.

"Simple," the man answers. "I couldn't get any celery."

11. A kangaroo walks into a bar and orders a drink. The bartender makes it, brings it over, and says to the kangaroo, "We don't get too many animals around here."

To which the kangaroo answers, "And at these prices, you won't see me in here any more either."

12. A drunk is walking down the street when he bumps into his friend. He tells him, "I bet I can prove to you that I'm Jesus Christ."

The friend says all right, here's five dollars. The drunk turns and walks into a nearby bar. And just as they're both going to sit down, the bartender turns around and says, "Jesus Christ, are you in here again?"

13. A drunk goes into a bar and he's so plastered he can hardly stay on the barstool. He asks for a drink and the bartender refuses, saying the man's too drunk to be served. The drunk gets hostile and replies well if I'm drunk, then you're ugly. "Gimme a drink." The bartender sticks to his guns and still refuses. So does the drunk, who keeps calling him ugly. Finally the drunk tires out and decides to go, saying, "You're probably right, I am drunk. But tomorrow I'll be sober. And you'll still be ugly."

14. A man noticed a sign on the window of a bar saying, "All the beer you can drink for one dollar. He went in and said, "That sounds like a good deal. I'll take two dollars' worth."

15. A man walked into a bar with a pig under his arm. "Where on earth did you find that filthy animal?" asked the bartender.

"Oh, him? I bought him at an auction," replied the pig.

16. A man walks into a bar carrying a door. "Why are you carrying that door?" asked the bartender.

"Well, last night, I lost my keys, so I'm carrying around the door in case somebody finds them and tries to break into my house."

Said the barman, "What happens if you lose the door?"

Man: "Oh, that's okay. I left the window open just in case."

17. A man walks into a bar and orders three doubles, which he promptly swallows in three gulps and then keels over.

"That's what I like about John," said the man next to him on the stool. "He certainly knows when he's had enough."

18. Pat and Mick worked in a brewery. One day they were cleaning out one of the heavy vats when Pat fell in and drowned. Mick had to deliver the sad news to Pat's widow.

"Did he suffer much?" she inquired.

"No, I don't think so," Mick answered, "except that he had to come out twice to go to the bathroom."

19. A bartender got a job next to a deaf and dumb school, and in order to be able to handle his special customers, he had to learn the sign language for the drink names. He was doing fine until one night around midnight when he couldn't interpret the signs the people were making. Frantically, he made up one drink and then another, but they just kept shaking their heads as if dissatisfied. Finally the exasperated bartender called up the bar owner and told him that he just couldn't figure out the strange signs the customers were making.

"Oh that," replied the owner. "I told them time and time again, that no singing was allowed in the bar."

20. Two fellows were drinking in a pub one night. One was a hunchback and the other was a cripple. It was getting late and the hunchback decided to take a shortcut through a cemetery on his way home. When he did, he ran smack dab into a ghost. The scared hunchback didn't know what to do at first. Then the ghost spoke, "What's that thing on your back?" he asked, and continued, "I'd like to have it."

With that he removed the hump, and the grateful fellow was

cured. The next night the former hunchback returned to the bar and told the people his incredible story.

The cripple was so impressed he decided to take the same shortcut and see if he, too, could find the miracle ghost. The cripple started walking through the cemetery and lo and behold, the ghost appeared.

The ghost said, "What's that on your back?"

To which the cripple replied, "Nothing."

Then the helpful ghost answered, "Here, why don't you take this."

21. Two men sat talking in a bar. "Did you make it home all right last night?" the first asked the second.

The second man replied: "I was doing fine until I got to the corner, then somebody stepped on my fingers."

22. The bartender looked up and saw a pink elephant, a green rat, and a yellow snake all sitting at the bar. "You're a little too early, boys," he said. "He hasn't shown up yet."

23. "Boy," said the drinker to himself, while recalling the night before, "that was a great party while I lasted."

24. Two drunks watched a stout lady get on a scale, place her coin in the slot, and wait for her correct weight. But the scale was broken and it only registered fifty pounds. "Gosh!" said one to the other "She's hollow."

GLOSSARY

Abricotine—A French apricot liqueur.

Advokaat—An eggnog-tasting liqueur from Holland.

Ale—A brew made out of malt that is darker and more bitter than beer. Contains about 6 percent alcohol.

Almondrado—A Mexican almond liqueur.

Amaretto—An almond-flavored liqueur from Italy.

Anisette—A licorice-flavored liqueur from Italy.

Apple-flavored brandy—An apple liqueur.

Aquavit—A Danish liqueur made from caraway seeds and other flavorings.

Arrack rum—An Oriental drink, high in alcoholic content, made from rice.

Bacardi—A Cuban liqueur made principally from rum.

Beer—A liquor fermented from malt flavored with hops and cereals. Alcoholic content about 6 percent.

Benedictine—A brandy-based, herb-flavored liqueur. Originally created by a Benedictine monk, the recipe still remains a carefully guarded formula.

Benedictine and Brandy (B and B)—A French liqueur made from aromatic herbs.

Ben Shalom—An orange-flavored liqueur from Israel.

Bitters—A spicy, hot mixture used in drinks for flavoring.

Café Benedictine—A blend of coffee liqueur and Benedictine.

Café Orange—A combination of coffee and orange liqueurs.

Calisay—A quinine-flavored liqueur from Spain.

Chartreuse—A liqueur that's a combination of herbs and spices made in France by the monks of the Carthusian order. It comes in yellow or green.

Cheri-Suisse—A liqueur flavored with chocolate and cherries.

Cherry Blossom liqueur—A cherry-flavored liqueur from Japan.

Cherry Heering—A cherry-flavored liqueur from Denmark.

Cherry Rocher—A cherry-flavored liqueur from France.

Choclair—A coconut- and chocolate-flavored liqueur from the U.S.

Cocktail—A lightly alcoholic drink served before lunch or dinner. It's made with all of the basic liquors in a 1 to 5 to 1 proportion.

CocoRibe—A coconut- and rum-flavored liqueur from the Virgin Islands.

Cointreau—An orange-flavored liqueur.

Collins—A popular summertime drink made in tall glasses with either gin, rum, brandy, or whiskey; sugar; lemon or lime juice; and club soda.

Cooler—Another summertime favorite, served in a well-iced, tall glass with any of the basic liquors, sugar, lemon juice, and club soda.

Cordial-Medoc—A French liqueur made from a blend of oranges, brandy, cherries, and crème de cacao.

Cranberry—A liqueur made from cranberries.

Crème de bananes—A liqueur made from bananas and brandy.

Crème de cacao—A liqueur made from cocoa beans, vanilla, and spices. It comes in either white or brown.

Crème de cassis—A French liqueur made from black currants.

Crème de cerise—A cherry liqueur from France.

Crème de fraises—A strawberry-flavored liqueur.

Crème de menthe—A brandy- and mint-flavored liqueur which comes in white, red, and green.

Crème de moka—A liqueur made from coffee beans and brandy.

Crème de noyau—An almond-flavored liqueur made from peach and apricot pits.

Crème de Recco—A liqueur made from brandy, sugar, and tea leaves.

Crème de vanille—A liqueur made from vanilla beans and brandy.

Crème de violette—A liqueur with the taste and smell of violets.

Curaçao—A West Indian liqueur made from the peels of curaçao oranges and other spices. It comes in green, white, orange, and blue.

Drambuie—A Scotch-based liqueur with an added base of honey, herbs, and other spices.

Fior dell'alpi—An Italian liqueur made from herbs and spices.

Fizz—A popular daytime drink made with gin, whiskey, wines, or rum; sugar, lemon or lime; club soda, and egg white.

Flip—A light drink to be whipped up in a blender. It contains an egg, sugar, sherry or whiskey, and is served in a sour glass.

Forbidden Fruit—An apple liqueur.

Fraise—A brandy- and strawberry-flavored liqueur.

Framboise—A brandy- and raspberry-flavored liqueur.

Frappe or On the rocks—Any of your favorite alcoholic beverages poured over ice in a cocktail (frappe) or old-fashioned (on-the-rocks) glass.

Galliano—An Italian liqueur flavored with anise and vanilla.

Goldwasser—A brandy-based, herb-flavored liqueur with tiny specks of gold leaf in it.

Grand Marnier—A cognac-based, orange-flavored liqueur.

Highball—The most basic drink a bartender can make with one of the standard liquors and a mixer.

Irish Mist—A liqueur made with Irish whiskey, honey, and orange.

Kahlúa—A Mexican coffee- and vanilla-flavored liqueur.

Kirsch—A liqueur made from wild black cherries.

Kümmel—A liqueur made from caraway seeds.

Light whiskey—A spirit distilled at a high proof and then blended with other aged neutral spirits.

Liqueur jaune—An option to yellow Chartreuse.

Liqueur verte—An option to green Chartreuse.

Lochan Ora—A Scotch whiskey-based liqueur flavored with herbs.

Malt—A sprouted barley used in making Irish and Scotch whiskeys.

Mandarine—A cognac-based, orange-flavored liqueur from France.

Maraschino—A sweet liqueur flavored with cherry and almond.

Mazarine—An Argentinian herb-based liqueur.

Midori—A melon-flavored Japanese liqueur.

Mirabelle—A plum-flavored liqueur.

Noyau—A brandy-based liqueur flavored with fruits and bitter almond.

Ojen—A Spanish anise-flavored liqueur.

Orgeat—An almond-flavored nonalcoholic syrup.

Ouzo—A Greek anise-flavored liqueur.

Parfait amour—A sweet French liqueur flavored with herbs, spices, fruits, and brandy.

Pasha—A Turkish coffee-flavored liqueur.

Passionola—A passion fruit-flavored, nonalcoholic syrup.

Peach liqueur—A brandy-based liqueur flavored with peaches.

Pear liqueur—A Hungarian liqueur made from pears.

Peppermint schnapps—A mint-tasting liqueur.

Pernod—A licorice-flavored American liqueur.

Peter Heering—See CHERRY HEERING.

Picon—A bitters from France, made with oranges, quinine, and gentian.

Pineapple liqueur—A Caribbean liqueur flavored with pure pineapple.

Prunelle—A plum-flavored liqueur.

Punch—The ideal party beverage usually made with a gamut of liquors, mixers, and fruits.

Quetsch—A natural liqueur made from the juice of fermented prunes.

Quince brandy—A brandy-based liqueur made from quince and spices.

Quinquina—An aromatic wine flavored with herbs and quinine.

Rock and rye—A rye whiskey-based liqueur mixed with fruit juice and rock candy syrup.

Roiano—An Italian liqueur flavored with vanilla and anise.

Roncoco—A rum- and coconut-flavored liqueur.

Sabra—An Israeli liqueur flavored with orange and chocolate.

Sake—A Japanese liqueur made from fermented rice.

Sambuca—An Italian liqueur with an anise flavor.

Sangria—A punch made of red wine and fruit juices.

Sciarada—An Italian orange- and lemon-flavored liqueur.

Slivovitz—A Yugoslavian plum brandy.

Sloe gin—A liqueur made from sloe berries and gin.

Sour—An anytime drink made of whiskey, rum, brandy, or gin mixed with lemon juice and sugar.

Southern Comfort—An American whiskey-based liqueur flavored with peaches.

Strawberry liqueur—A liqueur made from strawberries.

Strega—An Italian liqueur made from herbs and spices.

Swedish punsch—A rum-based liqueur combining spices and citrus flavors.

Tia Maria—A Jamaican coffee-flavored liqueur.

Tiddy's—A Canadian whiskey-based liqueur.

Triple Sec—A sweet, orange-flavored, brandy-based Italian liqueur.

Tuaca—An Italian liqueur flavored with brandy, citrus, and milk.

Vaklova—A vodka-based liqueur flavored with herbs.

Van der Hum—A liqueur from South Africa.

Vandermint—A chocolate-mint liqueur from Holland.

Wild Turkey liqueur—A bourbon-based liqueur.

Yukon Jack—A Canadian liqueur flavored with herbs and citrus.